THE KIM
KARDASHIAN
PRINCIPLE

THE KIM KARDASHIAN PRINCIPLE

Why

Shameless

Sells

(and How to

Do It Right)

JEETENDR SEHDEV

piatkus

PIATKUS

First published in Great Britain in 2017 by Piatkus

1 3 5 7 9 10 8 6 4 2

A CIP catalogue record for this book
is available from the British Library.

ISBN 978-0-349-41298-6

Printed and bound in Great Britain by
Clays Ltd, St Ives plc

Papers used by Piatkus are from well-managed forests
and other responsible sources.

Piatkus
An imprint of
Little, Brown Book Group
Carmelite House
50 Victoria Embankment
London EC4Y 0DZ

An Hachette UK Company
www.hachette.co.uk

www.improvementzone.co.uk

To my loving parents, Vijay Laxmi and Harjit Sehdev.
Thank you for my guiding principles in life.

Contents

Acknowledgments

Thank you God for testing me every day and giving me the strength to make this book a reality. Thanks to my mother and my family for their unconditional love, support and putting up with my insanity. This would not have been possible without you. Thanks to my biggest fans, Richa and Aakash, and to my audiences around the world for their amazing support over the years.

I'd like to thank my visionary publishing teams at both St. Martin's Press, including George Witte, Sally Richardson and Emily Carleton, and Little, Brown books, including Jillian Young and Meri Pentikäinen. Thank you for the opportunity, your patience and believing in me. I'd also like to thank my stellar team at UTA.

Melissa Magnus for visiting; Paul Wassgren for the pizza; Sally Hotchkin for always being there; Anne-Marie Cecconi for kicking ass; Kim Rushton because some things were meant to be; Leslie Noye and Matthew Sachs for your brilliant minds; Anne Donohoe for being my partner in crime; Angela and Art for my home away from home; Martin Sorrell for the opportunity; Steve Burke for the inspiration; Jeffrey Wilson,

Robert K. Silverstein, Jonathan Wald, and Genevieve Wong for your calls; and Leland Stephen for keeping me out of trouble. Oh, and last but not least, thank you, Kim Kardashian West. ;)

THE KIM
KARDASHIAN
PRINCIPLE

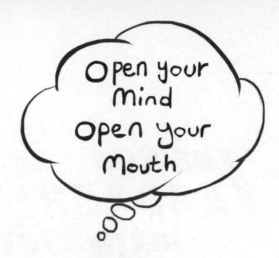

Introduction

Let's do some "we shouldn't be doing this" things.

So what *is* the Kim Kardashian Principle (KKP)? It's breaking through by becoming your own champion. It will help you and your ideas connect with today's audiences, who are radically different from their predecessors. It won't be easy, though. It takes time and energy to unlearn deeply ingrained attitudes and behaviors and truly open your mind to seeing the world in a different way. The KKP requires you to both use reason *and* acknowledge emotions. It requires you to be brave enough to follow through and act on your convictions. Once you take the plunge, it's worth it. It's effective as well as empowering to say, and mean, "This is who I am, this is what I believe, and this is what my idea is about. Love it or leave it!"

Ideas, products, services, and people that follow the Kim Kardashian Principle are the ones that will break through against all odds, at all costs, and come out on top—just like Kim. These ideas don't traffic in shame and have little regard for the judgment of others. They exude authenticity, and, ultimately, they define the culture. The KKP isn't just about breaking the rules; it's about creating your own rules. It's not about living up to other people's standards but living up to your own standards. The principle demands that you be so true to who you are and what you believe—at all times—that you can't help but convey your DNA to everyone you touch.

Why Should You Listen to Me?

The best way to find out if you can trust somebody is to trust them.

—ERNEST HEMINGWAY

My name is Jeetendr Sehdev, and I'm the world's leading celebrity branding authority—think your typical showbiz TV host, but with more book smarts and a much sharper jawline. What does it mean to be a celebrity branding authority? Simply put, I know a lot about celebrities, brands, and what people *really* think of them. I spend my mornings teaching marketing at the University of Southern California, my afternoons advising blue-chip brands about strategic alliances with celebrities, and my evenings talking pop culture on prime-time TV, from *Access Hollywood* to CNN. *Forbes* magazine describes me as a "real mad man," *Variety* calls me "the best in the business," and *US Weekly* magazine calls me "Hollywood's new phenom." Who am I to argue?

I've been in the spotlight in a big way over the past five years, but it's taken a lifetime to develop my methodology and a massive amount of self-belief to get out there and speak my mind. I reveal what people really think about celebrities, and I advise brands which of them to partner with if they want to be taken seriously. In fact, I'm the only person who's talking about celebrities in the media with some level of rigor and intelligence. But that's just one reason you should listen to me.

Over the course of my career, I've done everything from advising ultra-high-net-worth individuals at JP Morgan to consulting with the world's most prestigious companies on their business challenges. I was hired and mentored by advertising tycoon Sir Martin Sorrell at WPP, where I helped develop and direct iconic brands like American Express. I worked at all the right companies and checked all the right boxes—including graduating from Oxford and Harvard. But I found that no one at any of those places had all the answers, and I knew there had to be something bigger.

I'm telling you all this to underscore the new reality that birthed this book: traditional ways of connecting with people have now gone out the window, and in order to change the way we think about products, services, and ideas, we've got to change the way we think about ourselves. Forget the rigid ideas that were passed down to you by the old guard and are holding you back. No longer is the world black or white—it comes in shades of gray, and Millennials and Generation Z are leading the way. Focus on what you believe and what you want to create, regardless of the blowback. The old approaches no longer work, so you've got to blaze your own trail.

Kim Kardashian? You Can't Be Serious

> It's a skill to get people to really like you for *you*, instead of a character written for you by somebody else.
>
> —KIM KARDASHIAN

Why the Kim Kardashian Principle? Because Kim Kardashian has indisputably shaped our culture and the way it unfolds; she is a grand-scale indicator of how to behave if you want to achieve certain goals. Her stunning popularity represents a seismic shift in the way ideas catch on and how people, products, and services can capitalize on this change to build stronger, more intimate connections with consumers. The megamix of vulnerability, narcissism, and sheer audaciousness that has propelled Kim from reality-show laughingstock to cover girl and social media superstar is a force to behold.

By reading this book, you'll understand how to do in your own life and business what Kim does on such a grand scale. Be brave enough to dig deeper than the conventional wisdom, and be honest about what you *really* think and feel—don't waste time worrying about what you think you should think and feel. Be authentic about everything—from the way you interact with others to the way you present ideas or build product lines.

Is tomorrow's world a new one in which anything goes? I believe it is. It's certainly a world in which people want to proclaim who they are and to believe in themselves more than anything else. Be brave enough to embrace this change. Know that you no longer get taken seriously by savvy audiences by fitting into a neat box and following conventional wisdom. If you want to really break through, you've got to find your own freedom. If that makes you uncomfortable, don't worry. There will always be someone there to tell you who to be, how to think, and how to behave—if you let them.

The Six Principles of SELFIE

I'd give my right arm to be ambidextrous.

—YOGI BERRA

My philosophy and methodology are based on science and art, left brain and right brain. In this book, I paint with a broad brush. I use examples from the business world, history, pop culture, science, and my own experience to show you how to succeed by championing yourself and your ideas. I'm not condoning any particular way of life; this methodology can work for anyone. You just have to be willing to make the leap.

The new-world celebrities of Millennials and Generation Zers, like Kim Kardashian, are canaries in a global, *TMZ*-fueled coal mine. Why *wouldn't* you study the way they interact with and influence their fans? After all, if you want your ideas or products to be loved, obsessed over, and shared, then you need to follow the lead of the most loved, obsessed over, and shared celebrity there is—Kim Kardashian. The six principles of SELFIE will maximize the effect of everything—your personal brand, product innovation, policy initiatives, and marketing campaigns. Your ideas will break through and catch on like wildfire.

SURPRISE
EXPOSE
LEAD
FLAWS
INTIMATE
EXECUTE

SURPRISE

Admit it: you thought Kim Kardashian was a joke at first. After all, she didn't exactly look or act the part. California sex symbols are blond and blue-eyed. These old-school glamazons fit a mold, one that would shatter into a million pieces if our girl KK tried to squeeze into it. Yet shattering the mold turned out to be her greatest accomplishment. Ideas that want to break through in today's crowded and disengaged marketplace have to follow Kim's lead, finding their distinguishing characteristic and amping it up—even if it seems to go against marketing orthodoxy. Be unique and innovative—and make no apologies.

EXPOSE

Consumers are instantly suspicious of caveats, halfheartedness, and pivots. The Kardashians have stayed relentlessly true to who they are, and this has allowed them to weather all kinds of should-be scandals, including a transgender father, question-able product endorsements, and multiple failed marriages. Kim rarely holds anything back, for any reason. And this is a cru-cial lesson for ideas and individuals that want to connect today. It's better to be overexposed than edited. Have the courage of your convictions. Don't pull punches.

LEAD

Kim Kardashian is an entirely self-made creature; she didn't succeed in the Paris Hilton era but instead remade the mod-ern celebutante in her own image. Remaking culture is a risky business, an all-or-nothing game. You may be mocked or—worse—ignored, but if you have conviction, your audi-ence will eventually align with your vision. Don't tap into the existing culture—*create* it. Establish new norms and rally people to your vision. Show the world your version of the future.

FLAWS

Let's be perfectly clear: Kim Kardashian is an utterly flawed individual, and so are you. She built her fortune on one (liter-ally) massive flaw—her well-endowed derriere—turning it into a million-dollar asset. She took her suburban sensibili-ties and lack of education and reframed them as modern so-phistication and glamour. And, most notoriously, she used her leaked sex tape (which she strongly denies she leaked) as a springboard to overnight fame and lasting success. Any idea that wants to connect with consumers has to proudly and boldly showcase its flaws. Consumers are bored with—and in-different to—perfection. Flaws are revolutionary, intoxi-cating, and compelling, so embrace yours.

INTIMATE

Kim is so much more than just a pretty face on Instagram. She's an entrepreneur with her own beauty products; a fashionista and walking billboard for designer labels; she has a game app and emojis. She's also a wife, mother, and sister, as well as a cybermate to millions. Being many things in one bodacious package endears her to many different people and has helped her create intimate relationships with a legion of fans around the world, across old and new media. Ideas that want to generate a similar level of intimacy will need to redefine old-school notions of exclusivity. One size no longer fits all, so make sure your ideas and messages are tailored and focus on providing practical value and additional benefits.

EXECUTE

Kim doesn't sit around waiting for things to happen to her; she goes out and makes them happen. Today, execution needs to be an integral part of any framework. I've learned to live the principles of SELFIE, and so should you. Let's get started.

CHAPTER 1

How I Arrived at the Kim Kardashian Principle

Jeetendr Sehdev is a cyborg who thinks all human beings around him exist solely as brands.

—GAWKER MEDIA

*T*here may be some truth to that comment, but my journey from buttoned-up British schoolboy to celebrity authority to so-called cyborg has been far from simple. And if I wasn't doing something right, I wouldn't be getting noticed in Hollywood.

My fascination with celebrities goes back to my childhood in Bristol, England, where I grew up obsessing over everyone from Duran Duran to Wacko Jacko with an intensity that, quite frankly, confused my down-to-earth, Indian-born parents. Back then, celebrities really were larger than life—skinny ties, big hair, and world-conquering attitudes. My formal education began at Amberley House School, a British preparatory school where I learned the little book of English etiquette, paid attention during my Latin lessons, and developed a love for public speaking in my drama classes. But it wasn't until my father took ten-year-old me on a spur-of-the-moment trip to Los Angeles that I found my calling—the one that determined the course of my life.

When I returned to England, I attached a poster of the City of Angels, with a crystal-clear view of the city skyline and the Hollywood sign, over my bed. Every night, I escaped to Hollywood, if only in my mind, to survive the bullying at Colston's, my all-boys secondary school. I knew I had to break free from the rigid, hierarchical, "character-building" world in which I was trapped. I needed to get back to L.A. One day, with my face smashed against the wall, receiving my fifth wedgie of the week, it dawned on me—at the moment the elastic snapped—that one way I could get to California was to become a plastic surgeon. Despite a brief detour into runway modeling (we all have our moments), I stayed on track and went to Bristol University to pursue a career in medicine. But after my first behind-the-scenes look at the UK's distinctly unglamorous National Health System, I realized that my desire to heal others was misplaced.

Instead, upon graduation, I pivoted 180 degrees and decided to become a power banker, knowing it would allow me to travel far and wide, shop on Jermyn Street (look it up), and live my idea of the high life. I lasted about five minutes on the trading floor, and promptly requested a transfer to the private wealth division of JP Morgan, where I soon found myself mingling with members of the British elite. After two years, just shy of my twenty-fourth birthday, I'd had my fill of polo matches and auction houses and was ready for a little more substance, so I turned to the world of consulting and started learning about the inner workings of a range of Fortune 500 companies. As a management consultant, I learned a lot, but after a few years of number crunching and data forecasting, I was more than itching to exercise the creative side of my brain and return to the world of academia, so off I went to Oxford University to study history.

I was still determined to get to Hollywood, but what was left? I'd rejected medicine, banking, business consulting. Surely there was something that would get me there. In the last week of my finals at Oxford, after watching the Joe Pesci movie *With Honors*, shot at Harvard University, I decided my next stop would be Cambridge, Massachusetts, to get my MBA. No, it wasn't L.A., but it was three thousand miles closer than England. It's true, I went to Harvard to get to Hollywood, which makes about as much sense as the rest of this story.

I left with an MBA and a coveted offer at advertising agency Ogilvy & Mather in New York City. I was home at last, metaphorically speaking, and branding was the key to unlocking the door—the perfect combination of art, science, and business. It was a coming-of-age of sorts, and while I still had my sights on the West Coast, I loved my fifth-floor walk-up in NOLITA (despite the bathtub in the kitchen), and knew that I was finally on my way.

After a year at Ogilvy, I dropped a bombshell. I wanted to transfer to Los Angeles and work in celebrity public relations. My bosses were surprised to say the least, and they didn't believe my Ivy League education and work experience directing prestigious brands like American Express and Dove was quite the right fit for celebrity PR. Besides, they had gotten used to me working 25/8 and wooing big clients. But I was determined. I knew there was more to the red carpet than most people believed (i.e., it wasn't just superficial, soul-destroying, himbo work), and I was determined to prove it. Besides, there's a *People* magazine whore in all of us.

Once in L.A., I began to get a glimpse of what I was *really* interested in—the inner workings and behind-the-scenes antics that powered Hollywood's biggest deals. Over the next several years at business meetings, in hotel bathrooms, on movie sets, and at award ceremonies, I received a crash course in business that neither Oxford nor Harvard could rival. All the rules that I'd learned about strategy, planning, reason, and rationality went out the window.

Emotion was everything in Hollywood. I saw a studio executive beg to have his latest crush cast in a TV show, an A-list actress fake her pregnancy because she couldn't afford to gain weight, and a teen heartthrob throw more than a tantrum because his manager forgot his steroids. I couldn't believe the gulf between their images and their actualities. These celebrities were brands. They had clearly defined identities that were the premise of their appeal. Just as a strong logo instantly communicates what a product is about, these celebrities' engineered characteristics, behavior, and words conveyed who they are. And just as a good brand makes an emotional connection with consumers, successful celebrities do the same.

Bringing these insights together with those I had learned from my banking, consulting, and advertising days, I embarked on a new journey of my own creation—celebrity branding. It was a radical approach: each celebrity as a unique brand, a unique product, and not just one of many generic actors, musicians, or athletes. I planned to base my work not only on empirical research and insight but also on my own intuition.

As I applied the research techniques of branding—focus groups, online surveys, regression analysis, and ethnographies—to celebrities, a methodology began to emerge, one that I not-so-modestly christened JAAM™ (Jeetendr's Alternate Aptitude Methodology) because it "jammed" together the skills usually divided between the right brain and the left brain into a powerful whole-brain way of thinking. Besides, having now studied the arts and the sciences, worked in banking and advertising, dated Oxonians and Angelenos, I had developed a rather ambidextrous brain myself, and I couldn't help but think in both scientific and artistic terms. Until I developed JAAM, marketers could only guess the influence of a celebrity based on their perceived star power (a poorly defined concept at best), or even worse, their number of Twitter followers. But my research revealed something contradictory: popularity does not translate into influence. Numbers are just a starting point, a platform from which you can investigate deeper truths by examining the psychological, motivational, and emotional needs of audiences—and what they respond to might surprise you.

Getting SELFIEd

And this is how I came to name the Kim Kardashian Principle. I realized that uncovering the truths about how people *really* build relationships with celebrities and how the most successful celebrities communicate with their fans could be marketing gold for anyone with an idea, product, or service to sell. Let me take you through my discovery of SELFIE, the six fundamentals of the principle.

I've always been more of a high tea than a hip-hop guy, so little did I know that an invitation to a party in the Hollywood Hills would change all that, not to mention net me a few death threats. At the bash, I noticed the DJ was playing everyone from artist A to B to C, but not artist Z. Of course, I'm talking about Mr. Shawn Corey Carter, also known as Jay Z. The music world had perpetuated an image of the rap star as phenomenally successful and equally influential, with extra points for bagging Queen Bey. But that perception didn't quite ring true at the bash and amid his target audience who prided themselves on being "real." I've rarely been fooled by the smoke and mirrors of Hollywood, but even I had assumed Jay Z was the king of hip-hop, so I was transfixed. I decided to investigate this odd discrepancy, in the name of better understanding hip-hop audiences and their relationship to celebrities. What I discovered was that, far from being influential, Jay Z was viewed as a phony, a sellout, someone who was no longer authentic.

In 2013, when this—my first big interview—was published in *Business Insider*, the reaction was immediate and visceral. The story went viral. Having surveyed a thousand Millennials, I had struck a nerve—a really raw one. While the media had been telling the world that Jay Z was the best thing since sliced bread, I had revealed the exact opposite. And it wasn't just my opinion, it was a demonstrable fact. The conclusion was simple but striking: staying true to your roots and keeping it real, by not having some sort of façade, is what resonates with audiences.

I was blown away by the public. I had never expected my

first interview to make headlines around the globe. Nevertheless, I was keen to use my newfound notoriety, and methodology, to examine other phenomena we take for granted. It was just a matter of time before I turned to the world of sport.

As a Brit, I've always been baffled by the rules of American football. The thought of drinking beer and watching players of the "big game" inflict their fellow countrymen with brain damage was a far cry from strawberries, champagne, and center court at Wimbledon. So I turned my attention to Super Bowl XLVIII and the selection of singer Bruno Mars as the half-time performer. Despite Mars's quick rise to fame, many questioned the NFL's decision. He wasn't a megastar like Madonna, Prince, or Michael Jackson (who performed in 1993, surrounding himself with 3,500 children—what could go wrong there?). However, despite the lukewarm sentiment, I believed Mars to be a clever choice. Apart from the fact that he's an amazing live act, Mars's performances are incredibly intimate. Rather than some distant, unapproachable star on a faraway stage, he seems to almost speak to each member of the audience as an individual. I was so confident in my opinion that I wrote a centerpiece for *Adweek* just before the event, commending the choice. They were brave enough to run it. Turns out, they were clever enough too. Mars proved to be a super hit for the Super Bowl, attracting 115.3 million viewers, the largest audience in the history of the event, and his performance was met with rave reviews. Mars proved, finally, that larger-than-life is out and intimacy is in, and woe betide the image or event manufactured by professionals—authenticity is the key.

I was now convinced that I was on to something. Debunking myths and exposing the truth was proving addictive. My friends started calling me "the truth teller" (a marginally more flattering term than cyborg), but I was just doing me, doing my best to process a rapidly changing world and shifting entertainment industry.

A trip back to London from glitzy L.A. never fails to provide a timely reality check. It usually comes in the form of my mother; however, this one came from my then-thirteen-year-old nephew, Aakash. Over dinner he asked me, if I was the world expert on celebrities, why wasn't I talking about *real* celebrities? He was referring, of course, to YouTubers. While conventional wisdom leads us to believe mainstream stars have more power, presence, and influence than their DIY counterparts, my nephew convinced me that a YouTube star's fame was of equal—if not greater—value, and that Millennials are far more likely to be influenced by these candid, honest, and relatable internet icons than more aloof mainstream celebrities. I decided to put his thinking to the test. The rest, as they say, is history. My study went viral, again, and I revealed how YouTube stars have become much more reliable influencers of Millennials than traditional celebrities.

YouTube celebrities were more engaging, relatable, and authentic than their mainstream counterparts because they're not products of the PR industry and Hollywood handlers. Almost as soon as the study was announced in *Variety*, the *Sunday Times* and *Ad Age*, I saw the industry shift before my eyes. Hollywood started to redefine celebrities to include digital influencers. My results not only demonstrated the sheer power of YouTube as a medium, but they also showed me the power of leadership. These new celebrities were leaders *because* they were raw and intimate, not in spite of it. They represent a new opportunity for brands that have the courage to lead with their hearts—to be real, no matter how awful it might look. YouTube CEO Susan Wojcicki seemed to agree and decided to build her VidCon 2015 keynote around it. I was honored.

I was bona fide hooked. I read magazines and newspapers,

watched talk shows, joined chat forums—anything for inspiration. I started applying the JAAM to corporate brands: I predicted the demise of the NFL within five years when interviewed by ESPN in September 2014. I kept fine-tuning my authenticity detector and seeing through superstar images to the reality behind them. And the idea caught on, in a big way. My social media following exploded; I was suddenly the go-to guy for commentary on stars, their images, and their antics.

Along with the love, however, came the hate. There were many who challenged my predictions, which included Ellen DeGeneres's success hosting the Oscars, Neil Patrick Harris's failure at the same gig, Justin Bieber's ability to turn his brand around, and the inevitable disaster of the Oprah Winfrey and Weight Watchers partnership, among others. I welcomed it all, including the radio silence after I was proven right.

While on a trip to the South of France, I received news of an impending royal wedding back home, which gave me another idea of how to explode myths with my methods.

Living in the good old US of A had changed my perspective on the royal family: specifically, while I once heralded them as national treasures, I now considered them tagalongs who cost more than they were worth ($46 million per year of taxpayers' money, to be exact). So when the latest royal, Kate Middleton, entered the household (after a wedding that cost the economy $6 billion), the Palace felt some pressure to prove her worth. It came in the form of a PR stunt called "the Kate Middleton Effect," a supposed windfall for the fashion industry worth an estimated $1.2 billion. Apparently, everything the princess touched in Topshop would turn to gold and sell out in seconds. Only there was a problem: I wasn't buying it—and judging by the unchanged style of hundreds of millions of women around the world, neither were they.

Having worked with the most influential fashion icons and brands in the world, I intuited that the Duchess of Cambridge's "effect" would be nowhere near the value being promoted. Sure enough, my research showed that Michelle Obama, America's first lady, was viewed as over ten times more influential in terms of style, and even Lauren Pope of *The Only Way is Essex* and Snooki of *Jersey Shore* fame beat out the duchess. Eek. In truth, Kate's financial impact was a fraction of the claimed amount, around $300 million. I set the record straight from here to Hamburg and from *USA Today* to *Marie Claire*.

But what I found just as fascinating as the audacity of the overstatement was the *why*. Kate was now one of the most famous women in the world and a literal princess . . . so why did she come up short when compared to the other fashionistas? The answer, as it always is in England, was the Queen. The Palace's mastermind had orchestrated an image of Kate as too perfect. Sorry, your royal highness, nobody believes or buys perfect today. Lesson learned? Show your flaws.

Truth teller to my friends, professor of celebrity to my students, and celebrity branding authority to the public—these are the results of living and breathing brands and celebrities day and night. Some thought I was both a celebrity and a branding authority, and they began acting as if I was. I started getting recognized at Ralph's, and it was a bit unnerving. I was known for putting influencers on the map, but in reality I had become an influencer myself. Either way, I was just doing me, and it felt good.

The next area I wanted to investigate was something I had been noticing ever since I arrived in Hollywood—and now, with my reputation firmly established and my British inhibitions fully shed, I was ready. I never quite got used to the very blond landscape of Los Angeles. Most people are blond, and if they aren't blond they want to be blond. And of course everyone wants to be, and stay, young. Coming from cosmopolitan cities like London and New York and living among people of all ages, races, and genders, I was fascinated by this need to fit a mold. Hollywood suffered from a true lack of diversity, not just in percentage of peroxide usage but in ethnicity, culture, and age. Where I had come from, the graceful and accomplished Helen Mirren was still a star, and brunettes definitely did it better. I set out to study diversity in Hollywood to see just how pervasive the lack of it onscreen really was, and my research revealed that showbiz is whitewashed both in front of the cameras and behind, from casting agents to writers to producers to actors. The industry also perpetuates an idea of beauty that is inherently racist, trapped in a vicious cycle of its own longstanding traditions, stereotypes, and business models. My opportunity here couldn't be clearer: surprise your audience by simply being different. Go darker, go grayer, go gayer, and stop hating yourself.

There's a reason "action" is the final word in a slate. Despite what my headmaster used to teach me about the pen being mightier than the sword, Hollywood shows me something different every day. None of the above discoveries and lessons are worth anything if they aren't executed upon. In showbiz, amid a sea of dreamers, those who take decisive action will be the winners.

Bombarded with airbrushed images rather than the actual faces of real people, I occasionally have to pinch myself to make sure I'm not dreaming. But this is my life. And few things have given me such a kick as the invitation from the British government to give a presentation on the culture of fame, or being asked to provide evidence at some of the highest-profile celebrity trials on the value of celebrity brands. That is, until

I was asked to join the United Nation's fight to raise awareness about and eradicate modern-day slavery by 2030. There are 30 million slaves in the world today, and modern-day slavery, including forced labor and human trafficking, occurs in every country. The buttoned-up British schoolboy hasn't completely left the old world behind quite yet, but I've come a long way from getting wedgies in the boys' bathroom. And I've used the very strategies outlined in this book to make it all happen. You can, too.

CHAPTER 2

Surprise

*Anyone who thinks there's safety in numbers
hasn't looked at the stock market pages.*

—IRENE PETER

For a city where people will do anything to stand out, Hollywood is, I realized ironically, full of those desperate to fit in. Tinseltowners have the same noses, the same six-packs, the same blowouts, the same bulimia, all driven by the same need to be seen as sex symbols. So when the *Today* show asked me to talk about why Ben Affleck attempted to hide the fact that he was descended from a slave owner, I wasn't surprised. I knew that Affleck didn't think the revelation was very sexy, so he pressured the producers of PBS's *Finding Your Roots* to cover it up. It was a bad move. Not only did Affleck violate the trust of his fans but, as I predicted, the show was finally suspended. Affleck wanted to fit in and be seen like everyone else, but he wasn't like everyone else. Call it peer pressure, label it cowardice, or just chalk it up to his lack of imagination. Many of us have been conditioned to believe it's easier, less painful, and certainly less surprising to be a generic commodity rather than a unique entity. But today there is a greater penalty to not owning your difference.

Those who buy the beaten-path approach to success—thanks to their all-American, Midwestern upbringing, their old-school agents, or their deeply troubled drama teachers—work hard to morph into the girl next door or the sex kitten, the steely secret agent or exotic villain—anything to get that one big break. The enormous pressure stems in large part from Hollywood's archaic ideals, which glorify Caucasian, Midwestern looks above all others and drive the resulting commoditization of beauty and casting. If you look like *this* you can be a leading lady, but if you look like *that* you can only be her bitchy friend. Only there's a white elephant in the room. This so-called star-making mentality of veneers and steroids, boob jobs and bleaching has produced far more hookers than heroes.

The need to conform is very human. Some of us do it to fit

a preapproved mold or be accepted by those around us. Others conform because it's just easier to do what everyone else is doing than to think for themselves. But what happens when audiences decide they've had enough? When the blue-eyed golden boy is out and the big-nosed black guy is in? When the bootylicious Armenian brunette with ethnic features is deemed more bangable than the bubbleheaded blonde? When the Latina promotes herself from the toilet-cleaner to the wedding planner? When the quirky likes of Tina Fey venture out from behind the scenes of *Saturday Night Live* to headline a movie while Kate Hudson flogs subscription activewear? What happens when there is so much uncertainty that the casting director doesn't know any better?

The Fine Art of Deviance

The greatest illusion is that mankind has limitations.

—ROBERT MONROE

Despite its dark connotations, the word *deviant* just means "different from what is considered to be normal."[1] And from the little girl who spoke too loudly or played too roughly to the boy who loved Barbie dolls, the deviants have always had a difficult road. We've been trained to see difference as dangerous, and the results—including shame, bullying,[2] and, in many cases, suicide[3]—are tragic.

In sixteenth-century Europe, the "marginal people" who threatened society were the poor. Once "the poor of Christ," beggars were now seen as cursed and a threat to respectable, settled people. The first prisons were created as "Houses of

Correction" for them,[4] and poverty became a moral crime as well as a personal weakness. Over in England, the Reformation (when the English church broke away from the Catholic church in Rome) also saw the persecution of the deviants who refused to obey the pope or the king.

America's witch hunts began thirty years before the infamous Salem witch trials in colonial Massachusetts in 1692.[5] They were actually less about people practicing black magic than they were about managing the petty disputes and simmering rivalries of life in small colonial towns. By the time the trials ended in Salem in 1693, twenty women had been executed. Yet these "witches" were nothing more than mouthy and opinionated women—the Kim Kardashians and Grace Helbigs of their day. Their only sin was being openly and unabashedly different—and perhaps naïve enough to think that reason would prevail and they wouldn't be punished for not conforming.

Regardless of their logic, dictators have always feared difference. Lily Bart, the famous protagonist in *The House of Mirth*, was rejected by her social circle when she refused to play the game of upper-class Manhattan life, and literally chose death over marrying a bore and settling down to breed. The Nazis were repulsed by the good-time boys of 1930s Berlin, and they destroyed them as soon as the regime secured its power base.[6] These boys (and girls) lived on the edges of "normal" German society and, along with other outsiders— Jews, Poles, Afro-Germans, Gypsies, and the disabled—served no purpose in Nazi Germany. Exterminating them was a logical decision for Hitler and his followers.[7]

The late David Bowie was a deviant, down to the last strand of his DNA. He loudly (and proudly) proclaimed himself gay while paradoxically walking hand in hand with his wife, Angie, and pushing a baby carriage, only to take it back and say he was a closeted heterosexual. He insisted on his right to constantly reinvent himself, shedding old personas as easily as snakeskin, and refused to categorize himself or explain what he was doing. It's easy to forget how hated Bowie was in the early 1970s, labeled a "faggot" and a "poof," yet he ultimately connected with millions of fans around the world and gave a few more million misunderstood schoolchildren permission to be their own baddest, realest, most self-obsessed selves.

Society tends to pick and choose which deviants to punish. This kind of discrimination has a type of twisted logic: by rejecting people because of their race, sexuality, religion, or mental health, the core of society remains intact and unified in their beliefs (or perhaps their fear). This might have been a useful tactic in more unsettled times, but throughout history deviance has always been an artificial construct designed to keep the disenfranchised in check.

We like to think that we've evolved since then, but the truth is that many people remain just as suspicious and hateful toward deviants as our forefathers were. We still look down upon the woman who knows exactly what she wants in bed and the born-again Christian who gets caught with his pants down in a parked car with a prostitute. Despite the progress made by the LGBTQ community, pressure to conform to gender norms still "produces significant anxiety, insecurity, stress and low self-esteem for both boys and girls, and both for 'popular' young people and those who have lower status in school."[8] Our society is used to labeling those who are deviant as a fag, slut, or freak. But who is to say what's "normal"?

One thing's for sure: if you're not OK with the freaky truth about what you do and why you do it, then why should anyone else be? It takes courage to really show your differences, but it's crucial for any product, idea, or service today. These differences are what help you break through, create noise, and

seed success. Our deviants are our true cultural innovators—
not that we always realize it at the time.

#CurryScentedBitch

> Be yourself; everyone else is already taken.
>
> — OSCAR WILDE

Hollywood isn't the only place where people think they need
to fit a mold. In the summer of 2014, I was invited to attend a
lavish birthday bash of a Bollywood film actor. Having been
raised on Indian cinema, I was aware of this industry icon and
was genuinely excited that he reached out. That is, until we
spoke on the telephone and he kept referring to himself as
the Indian Brad Pitt. I found it strange given he didn't look,
sound, or act anything like Pitt.

There is a big penalty to not owning and rocking your differences. For former One Direction singer Zayn Malik, punish-
ment came from controversial rapper Azealia Banks. Just hours
after Zayn released images for his new single "Like I Would,"
Banks shared a picture collage on Instagram and began what
was to be an epic rant. Zayn claimed to have been inspired by
the futuristic look of Disney's *Tron*, but Azealia disagreed,
posting mirror images from Zayn's video and her own work.
She wrote, "Damn, Zayn be mood boarding the fuck out of
me . . . I'm not mad about this though. Zayn is a cutie pie."

Zayn initially didn't respond to the twenty-four-year-old
rapper's claims but eventually tweeted, "No lies. I see you
reaching but I don't care." He followed up with a cheeky "My
@'s too good for you." The resulting Twitter tirade that Azealia
unleashed on the former boy-bander, calling him a "faggot,"

"paki," and "sand nigger," had her instantly trending world-wide. "Dude, I make better music than you. Simmer down with that fake white boy rebellion and that wannabe bieber swag. . . . Lol u a bitch nigger for even responding like that. Keep sucking this yung rapunxel dick u hairy curry scented bitch." Things got worse as she continued, "Imma start calling you punjab you dirty bitch. . . . You a dick rider for real for real. Ride this dick until the wheels fall off Punjab."

Banks was labeled racist and homophobic, but that assessment only skims the surface of another problem. In addition to potentially copying her video, Zayn seemed to have covered up his unique background. As a Muslim, the child of a white mother and a Pakistani father, he wasn't like the other members of One Direction, nor was he exactly eager to point those facts out. He had westernized his Islamic last name from Javadd Malik to just Malik while in One Direction before dropping it entirely when he started his solo career. "USA IS ABOUT TO TEACH YOU WHO NOT TO FUCK WITH!!" Azealia ranted, referring to Zayn's move to Los Angeles and Trump's plan to ban Muslims from entering America. "When your entire extended family has been obliterated by good ol' the U.S of A will you still be trying to . . . Act like a white boy pretending to be black?" Azaelia questioned. "Do you understand that you are a sand nigger who emulates white boys' renditions of black male hood? Do you know how lost and culture less [sic] you are?"

Zayn, who has no problem biting back in Twitter feuds with the likes of ex-band member Louis Tomlinson, DJ Calvin Harris, and music producer Naughty Boy, remained notably silent. Unlike the slew of fake celebrity Twitter wars designed to get attention, this one was for real. While Zayn's social media team worked behind the scenes to control the damage, Azaelia continued to speak her truth.

Had Zayn downplayed the fact he was a Muslim in an attempt to increase his popularity? With over half of Americans having an "unfavorable" opinion of Islam, and the most common words that Brits think of when they hear the word *Muslim* being *terror, terrorism*, and *terrorist*, why not downplay your identity?[9] My research shows that 82 percent of people feel Zayn was manipulating his image and covering up his Muslim identity for commercial gain. Of those, three out of five people see Zayn as more Pakistani than white. Seventy-five percent of people believe that Zayn could positively impact the public's perception of Muslims by speaking about his ethnicity, and three out of five people believe that by dropping his last name, he is actually doing Muslims a disservice.

Today, audiences judge you on your personal moral code and whether you put your unique self—or the opinions of others—first. They respond to people with a point of view, people who stand for something original, whether they agree or disagree. Azealia said what had not been openly discussed before, thoughts that were on many others' minds, and that's what struck a nerve.

When you don't dress like everybody else, you don't have to think like everybody else.

—IRIS APFEL

Science proves that conformity is the slowest form of suicide. The Asch experiment (a series of studies investigating if people yielded to a majority group and the resulting effect on their beliefs) shows that our desperate need to fit in is sometimes so pressing that we will go along with others in a group and give a wrong answer to a question we've already answered correctly as an individual.[10] The Bernie Madoff scandal reveals that joining the cool kids' club gives us such a powerful sense of security that we, meaning hundreds of clever financiers, can fall prey to a charismatic, but obvious, con artist. After all, who wouldn't want to join a group of investors that included the world's largest bank (HSBC), Elie Wiesel's Foundation for Humanity, and Dreamworks CEO Jeff Katzenberg?[11] Perhaps most damagingly, when we give into conformity, we dupe ourselves into believing that imitation is the same thing as innovation and that copying ideas can be even more valuable than inventing them. The *Harvard Business Review* finds that many people who feel "different" try to hide their differences—such as ethnicity, sexuality, or family responsibilities—from each other.[12] Even white males "cover" by actively trying to hide their age, disabilities, or mental health issues. Almost 30 percent of professionals change their appearance, mannerisms, or speech to make their identity less obvious. That's a huge number, and a big shame. These instincts run contrary to our most authentic, exciting, and powerful creative endeavors. If you can't be honest with yourself, how will you ever convince your audience?

There Will Be Blood

Girls are superheroes. Who else can bleed for a week and not die?

If Ben Affleck, Bollywood, and Zayn Malik proved that homogeneity makes us lazy, culturally complacent, and kind of invisible, then my subway ride from CBS studios to my hotel in Manhattan one afternoon proved that being OK with the freaky truth about what you do, and why you do it, will definitely get you seen.

After eighty years of vague euphemisms, "blue liquid" advertising, and sex-segregated "growing up" talks, women clearly and suddenly said, "Fuck it." Blame it on Lena Dunham and the body-positive flesh-fest that is *Girls* or on Instagram provocateur Rupi Kaur, whose post of her fully clothed body and bloodstained pants and bedsheets were twice deleted by the app for "not following Community Guidelines."[13] Either way, five years into the fourth wave of feminism,[14] many feminine hygiene companies were still painfully out of touch with their audience (as recently as 2009, Kimberly-Clark's Kotex division was almost entirely staffed by men[15]). Given that the average woman in the Western world spends a minimum of $3,000 on her period over a lifetime and also introduces her daughters to "her" brand (which they generally remain loyal to), it's worth paying closer attention to this customer.

In early 2016, Thinx Underwear launched its first ad campaign that was primarily marketed on subway posters in New York City.[16] The product was an entirely new concept; period-proof panties that used four layers of fabric to absorb up to six teaspoons of blood at a time. The first layer removes moisture, the second is stain resistant and antimicrobial, the third functions like a pad, and the fourth is leak resistant.[17] The washable and reusable briefs and thongs were designed by women to be sustainable and environmentally friendly. It was also the first truly disruptive idea in period maintenance since the tampon (as we know it, created in 1931; as a concept, it's been around since the fifth century BCE[18]). Now all Thinx had to do was let potential customers know about this radical "re-thinking" of feminine hygiene.

Thinx had a clear message, but a not-too-substantial budget of $300,000 for 15,000 subway ads.[19] Alas, Outfront

Media, the firm that manages advertising within the New York City subway system, found the ads too direct for its liking. While they had no problem with cosmetic surgery ads for breast enlargement that used images of women holding grapefruits up to their chests, they found Thinx's use of both the word *period* and a grapefruit (albeit to represent a vagina in this case) more objectionable. Refusing to conform to existing menstrual market norms and ignoring Outfront Media's advice to "not . . . make this into a women's rights thing," Thinx took to social media. The outrage was swift, the awareness was immense, and the engagement was massive. And a few days later, the unaltered ads were all over the subway.

Thinx's plan worked on two levels. By owning the issue in a truly unique way, the company kick-started a conversation about menstruation that went viral, and by sharing the behind-the-scenes exchange, they made the MTA's outdated ideas about periods *every* woman's problem.[20] Thinx, in both idea and approach, was fundamentally different from its competitors in the feminine hygiene space: they candidly addressed menstruation and created a unique solution—absorbent, reusable underwear.

Miki Agrawal, owner and innovator of Thinx, sees further applications; next up are panties for women suffering from post-childbirth incontinence and a "bidet scrubber" to eventually replace environmentally catastrophic toilet paper. For each pair of Thinx underwear sold, the company sends funds to AFRIpads, an organization that teaches women in developing countries to make and sell reusable cloth pads. Women are empowered as entrepreneurs, and girls are able to purchase a sustainable quantity of pads at a reasonable price (and very often stay in the schools they may have left during the times they were menstruating and lacked affordable supplies).[21] So yes, embracing differences can be messy, but it's also a huge opportunity.

Thinx's deviance, down to the last strand of its DNA, resulted in phenomenal success—in three weeks, the company sold the number of self-absorbing panties it initially projected to sell in a year and a half. Its megacompetitors—such as Kotex's U brand, which ran commercials poking fun at the images in old-school feminine-hygiene ads, and Always, which launched its "Like a Girl" campaign to empower girls but failed to mention their relevant futures as menstruating women—still looked to fit in rather than stand out. These brands thought they were doing the right thing by playing along society's party lines. They positioned the (actually painful and messy) experience of periods as somewhat pleasant, or at least harmless. But this very attempt to normalize their products revealed their true inner thinking: periods were a dirty little secret. Audiences today punish ideas for abiding by party lines, especially when playing by the rules comes with the cost of consumers feeling sanitized and silenced. The power of surprise not only prevents your idea from disappearing into a sea of sameness but it can also stop it from being sidelined by the yes-men.

Whether it's "free-bleeding" outside the Houses of Parliament to protest the fact that tampons are subject to a luxury tax in the UK,[22] employers who are increasingly offering paid time off for women during their periods,[23] or YouTube star Ingrid Nilsen grilling Obama about why tampons are taxed as a luxury in forty states (he guessed that the legislators who made that decision were "most likely men"),[24] there's no shame in Millennials' game about their monthly cycle. Thinx used the power of surprise at each touch point of the brand, from the product idea's inception all the way through to its name and expression in advertising, and it continues to embrace its deviance with its latest conversation around *"Period-proof underwear that won't leak through your Tinder date (or Bumble or Grindr or Farmers Only). #NotAnAd #Ad."* In fact, the power of surprise helped Thinx turn the menstrual cycle "curse" into a blessing—a sign of a functioning, healthy body and a radical symbol of feminine independence.

Diversity Makes Ideas Innovative

If you're thinking like everyone else then you're not thinking.

—FRANK ZAPPA

One of the first things I tell my students at USC is that if you want to be a great innovator—or, at the very least, someone with a unique perspective on the world—then you have to surround yourself with difference. It's what's driven my interest in both the sciences and the arts, led me to date both Oxonians and Angelenos, brought the power of thinking from Harvard to Hollywood, and allowed me to create the area of celebrity branding. I've always been willing to be a little uncomfortable and a lot out of my depth or to be the only person who thinks (or looks) like me in the room. But it often runs counter to the natural human instinct: to find our tribes, or surround ourselves with "like-minded" individuals. As my students will tell you, "being questioned or constructively criticized may not always feel like a positive experience at the time, but it only leads to greater reflection on the how's and why's. A group of diverse thinkers leads everyone to see an idea in a new light."[25]

Millennials, especially, refuse to check their identities at the door. They believe in the value of their unique characteristics, and they want to bring that to the table. A team with members from diverse backgrounds and lifestyles may not see eye to eye on everything, but they'll most likely come up with powerfully resonant ideas. The lack of diversity in the Fortune 500—of race, gender, or sexuality—leaves them less able to innovate and more vulnerable to younger, nimbler companies, which generally embrace diversity. Research shows that firms with a focus on ideation see significant benefits if they have women and minorities in senior positions. And it's not just about creating a heterogeneous environment: companies that expect to do business around the world must promote and value diversity among their employees to create crossover ideas that can gain a competitive edge.[26]

The most successful ideas emerge when diverse minds from different backgrounds and disciplines come together. Apollo astronauts didn't wear space suits created by an aerospace contractor; they were designed by lingerie manufacturer Playtex, which knew how to fit the human body exactly. Die-hard gamers deciphered part of the molecular structure of HIV/AIDS that had stumped medical scientists for years. Lin-Manuel Miranda, creator of Broadway's hottest ticket *Hamilton*, brought the rhymes and rhythms of hip-hop to a biography of a founding father.[27] Harvard launched i-lab to bring students from all of its schools, undergraduate to graduate and professional, together on projects and businesses in which they may have shared interests but widely varied backgrounds and areas of expertise. One coalition of law, engineering, government, and chemistry postdoctoral students founded Vaxess Technologies, which discovered a way to stabilize vaccines for shipping and storage without refrigeration. Vaxess has over $6 million in funding, numerous awards, and grants from the National Science Foundation and the National Institute of Health.[28]

So if innovation is driven by diverse experiences, what does this mean for ideas that are going to connect with audiences today? Millennials see themselves as a group of truly diverse people, with different backgrounds and strengths. Their diversity isn't the moral or legal thinking of older generations; they reject that imperative as simple inclusion rather than actual diversity. You can't just put a black male and a white male who have similar backgrounds and who both attended Ivy League colleges on your team and expect innovation. Differences in race and gender alone aren't important diversifications— variations in life experiences, such as growing up in a different part of the country or world, and educational and work backgrounds are.[29] If you can show Millennials that you embrace them as they are, you will empower and engage them. Fail to consider their differences and needs, and you will lose them.

How Eyes on Screens Leads to Heads in Beds

The calendar? A mere convention.

—IRINA RATUSHINSKAYA

Like many in showbiz, I spend most of my time in a handful of celebrity-saturated boutique hotels where I'm sure my name is now engraved on the reservation roll. The scene is fun, but the service can suck. So I welcomed an invitation from Marriott International headquarters in Washington, D.C., to address their global marketing team on the latest thinking in branding and stayed at the Ritz Carlton to experience some real luxury. It was at the Marriott that I met charismatic crossover star David Beebe, VP of Global Creative and Content Marketing, and learned about his revolutionary plans to bring Marriott into the twenty-first century by changing the way the company marketed itself.

How do you corner the market when it seems that a shop

like yours sits on every street corner? That's a question Marriott had been tackling for a long time. How did the world's largest hotel chain, with 19 brands in 82 countries and more than 4,800 hotels, stay relevant in a cutthroat and rapidly changing travel market? The traditional industry formula for success, "Product + services & amenities + customer service = long-term loyalty, advocacy, and referral benefits,"[30] was proving less and less effective in light of Millennials' unique needs, and Airbnb had shaken up the industry by delivering on a more authentic travel experience.

Charged with the seemingly futile task of being "different," Marriott responded to its audience's changing needs by heading to Hollywood and hiring Beebe, a film and television producer whose innovative work in digital media was recognized by the Television Academy with two Emmy awards. On the surface it seemed like a bizarre move. Why would a hotelier be interested in a Hollywood maven? But in bringing on Beebe, the brand set in motion a revolution that would transform Marriott into a bona fide media company.

The risky move defied all conventional business wisdom. Marriott was not in the profession of media creation, but hospitality. The hotelier needed to stick to what it knew best—getting heads in beds. Its global marketing teams managed the creation of TV ads and traditional marketing, and the company had little experience in creative and content strategy. Some said Marriott was casting its net wide in an effort to stay relevant, whereas others believed the hotel chain faced an uphill battle, especially considering the plethora of travel programs, both on- and offline, and the sheer cultural challenges involved in producing this kind of material in-house. Even if the hotelier did get projects off the ground, how would they succeed? They wouldn't be able to own travel entertainment on-line, and audiences were at the leading edge of content creation.

There were, of course, elements of truth to the trash talk. Beebe had never worked in hospitality before, and D.C. was a far cry from the chilled-out culture of California. But that was exactly the opportunity. The in-house content team's value proposition was based on driving innovation through diversity in perspectives, diversity in culture, diversity in programming, and, last but not least, diversity in people. Beebe and his team would bring different skill sets and experiences to break through the competitive clutter and strengthen relationships with consumers.

Beebe launched the Marriott Content Studio, which was charged with developing, producing, and distributing creative content across all formats that both informed and entertained next-generation travelers. Marriott Content Studio's first film, *Two Bellmen*, is set in Los Angeles, but the JW Marriott Los Angeles is intentionally just a backdrop for the story of two rival bellhops who join forces to foil an art heist (inspired by Marriott's partnership with Christie's). *Two Bellmen* is a full-on Hollywood production, with actors from network television shows, music, dance, and a full production crew. The bellmen returned in *Two Bellmen Two*, venturing to the JW Marriott Marquis Dubai to save the day by returning a lost USB. Indian actress and L'Oréal spokeswoman Freida Pinto starred as the owner of the USB. The film also makes Dubai a character in its own right, highlighting its unique culture.[31] *Two Bellmen Three* was shot in Asia, with a wedding theme and an authentic Korean storyline.

Marriott property, the Paris Marriott Champs-Elysees Hotel, was the setting for the romance *French Kiss*. Renaissance Hotels produced both a film, *Business Unusual*, set in Chicago with a storyline focused on the business traveler, and *The Navigator Live* series featuring live musical acts at their hotels. Webisodes of *Courtyard Camera* captures NFL players making surprise visits to Courtyard by Marriott properties. Alongside the films, Beebe's team is also working with influencers to create content, like *Do Not Disturb* for the Millennial-focused Moxy Hotels brand, where YouTube talent Taryn Southern interviews her celebrity friends from a bed in the Moxy Hotel. The studio has also produced lifestyle programming like *Open Invitation*, with a focus on food and beverage. All of the content is meant to inspire travel within the viewer.

With Marriott Content Studio, the company was, for the first time, creating a direct value exchange between itself and its audiences—an important shift away from old-school marketing tactics. After all, nearly 90 percent of people watching shows on their DVR fast-forward the ads.[32] Marriott had pivoted to providing entertainment to consumers without trying to sell anything to them first. The idea behind it was that audiences don't think of a vacation, as they're planning it, through the lens of buying a hotel room but as a journey they're excited to take. Marriott wanted to be their companion along that entire journey. The films allowed audiences to experience various locations and decide whether or not they wanted to visit. The hotels appear in the films organically but are by no means the end point. This way Beebe empowered audiences to decide whether the city was one they wanted to visit—*and if Marriott was the hotel they wanted to stay at*. The company plans to create films for all of its brands and distribute them on YouTube and screen them in its hotels. The films will not only emphasize the distinctiveness of Marriott properties around the world but also the cultures that surround them.[33]

These projects were remarkably successful. *Two Bellmen* has garnered 5.1 million views on YouTube, *French Kiss* 6.1 million, and *Two Bellmen Two* had 1.5 million in its first week alone. Not only did the shorts capture the attention of Millennials in a cluttered market, but they also created fans of the brand and new customers of its hotels. They addressed the unique needs of the next generation of travelers—who "shun traditional ads and spend more time on YouTube and other digital platforms"—and presented entertainment with no overt branding, paradoxically creating "positive association with the brand so the next time (consumers) travel they will recall the time [it] didn't try to sell them anything."[34]

Marriott believed in innovation through diversity. The company brought Hollywood outsider Beebe into an industry that has been set in its ways since antiquity, and it considered its problems to be unique from those of other businesses. Beebe brought best practices from Hollywood to hospitality and opened the minds of the existing brand marketers to other ways of seeing things. The power of a diverse way of thinking got everyone to step up their game, blowing up business-as-usual operations and redefining ways of measuring success. The new culture embraced the fact that not everyone would see eye to eye and that this wasn't a weakness but a source of strength. The resulting innovation was so powerful that it infiltrated each touch point of the work, including the plot, cast, film structure, soundtrack, and locations, becoming the face of the brand. Marriott Content Studio is, in David Beebe's own words, "as creatively diverse as it is a safe place for the creative community, where we truly partner with creators to tell original stories that showcase our portfolio of 19 brands—positioning the hotels and destinations as characters themselves—ultimately inspiring viewers to travel."[35]

The Science of Diversity and Innovation

Normalness equals to sadness.

—PHIL LESTER

Several studies have shown that when we are placed in groups where everyone seems to be "like us," we assume that they already think like us. Instead of working hard to be creative— challenging, arguing, and sharing ideas—we put the bare minimum of effort into our work. Why do more when these like-minded individuals already share our POV? However, when a group contains members of different races, sexes, or any other kind of "other," suddenly we come to life. We no longer assume that we understand what the other person thinks. Instead we pay attention and work harder to communicate and innovate.

A study of over half a million patents demonstrates that innovators working alone are less likely to make significant breakthroughs and more likely to create lousy end products. "Collaboration can have opposite effects at the two extremes: it reduces the probability of very poor outcomes— because of more rigorous selection processes—while simultaneously increasing the probability of extremely successful outcomes" because of the multiplied possibilities available to diverse thinkers.[36] Racial and gender diversity have been shown to increase profits and market share in for-profit businesses, mostly by bringing groups that were once excluded back in.[37]

In one experiment on racial diversity and decision making, groups with racial diversity consistently outperformed all-white ones. A similar study finds that when a contrary idea is twice presented to a group of whites, it provokes more thought when presented by a black person than when introduced by a white person. A 2006 study on jury decision making finds white jurors become "more diligent and open-minded" when serving with black jurors. By contrast, all-white juries are less likely to thoroughly consider case facts and more likely to make errors recalling information.[38]

Being Bad (or, Sorry, Not Sorry)

Who gave this son of a bitch his green card?

—SEAN PENN

Since risky behavior seems to be de rigueur for Hollywood superstars, and brands often rely on their star power to engage fans, many chief marketing officers ask me how they can prevent a celebrity spokeperson's bad behavior from damaging their brand image. I often tell them that the real question we should be asking in today's digital age of transparency is, how can we strategically align ourselves with that devil-may-care attitude? Because being bad can be very, very good.

Soon after giving the opening keynote at the *Advertising Age* conference on the power of celebrity, I was e-mailed by the head of an international sports apparel company. One of their celebrity endorsers had tested positive for a banned substance, and they weren't sure whether to honor or cancel the athlete's contract. The endorsement wasn't as large as others in their portfolio, so they were tempted to play it safe by letting the noise die down and then decide on next steps. I suggested they do the opposite; they needed to show a zero-tolerance policy for doping, and publicly cut ties with the celebrity quickly. Why? Because in doing so, they would turn the potentially embarrassing situation into an opportunity. Audiences form opinions of you based on what you *don't* do as much as what you do. Within twenty-four hours, the company took action and got it right. Not only did the number of people who planned to buy their product spike but the perception of their company as one with integrity also hit a ten-year high. I've learned that covering up your true values in an attempt to keep the peace is never a good thing no matter how reasonable it may seem at the time.

Whatever Shia LaBeouf does, it's always unexpected and utterly true to his DNA. LaBeouf's behavior might drive his publicist insane in her attempts to maintain what was once his Disney-prince image, but it's his commitment to expressing his true nature that makes him fascinating. He spent much of the early 2010s redefining what a movie star and performance artist—and a bad boy—can be. Seemingly humbled after being accused of plagiarizing from an *Esquire* article in a tweeted apology for his sudden exit from a role in a Broadway show, Shia said "sorry" with a tweet that stole words from David Mamet, "invent nothing, deny nothing, speak up, stand up, stay out of school."[39] How apologetic can you really be if you use the very thing that got you into trouble in the first place in your (second, third, fourth, and so on) apology? Not very. LaBeouf threw himself into an extreme and prolonged act of "public penitence," this time with two artist collaborators. His L.A. performance art #IAMSORRY (during which he was allegedly raped by a female viewer) saw him sitting silent and motionless for long periods over the course of five days. A follow-up performance—2016's #ELEVATE—had him spending twenty-four hours in an Oxford University elevator, where he returned the physical assault favor, slapping a fan at his request as part of *his* experiential art piece.[40] LaBeouf also gave the performance of a lifetime (after all, he did find fame in the *Transformers* franchise) in Sia's 2015 "Elastic Heart" video, playing either a frustrated pedophile or the tortured caged animal, depending on your perspective. At least Shia was going after grown-ups when he grabbed Alan Cumming's leather-clad butt from the audience during a performance of *Cabaret*. Like Kanye, Miley Cyrus, and Justin Bieber, LaBeouf's preference for thinking and living out loud is key to his appeal. His bizarre, often unhinged behavior reveals the dangerous, destructive, and unbalanced urges that lurk within all of us, and we can't wait to see what he'll do next. The sum of LaBeouf's crazy actions suggests something more than a momentary impulse. He's bad, and he knows it.

People accuse me of being arrogant all the time. I'm not arrogant, I'm focused.

—RUSSELL CROWE

In 2011, I was racing back to my car after a lunch meeting in Beverly Hills when I saw former teenage heartthrob Charlie Sheen standing on the rooftop of the Live Nation building waving a machete and shouting "free at last." I don't believe I looked twice; at this point, it was just another day in Hollywood. Sheen had just been fired from his hit show *Two and a Half Men* and was in a free-fall of Playmates, porn stars, alcohol, and drugs; every day, it seemed, he made a new headline for his erratic behavior and disheveled, rambling personal appearances.[41] You would think that would have killed Sheen's endorsement potential, but not so; Fiat viewed him as a cash cow rather than a black sheep. It attached his wild behavior to the "bad boy" of its auto lineup: the Fiat 500 Abarth. The resulting commercial parodied Sheen's house arrest and connected his untamed character to Fiat's "racy" model—a move that appealed to people who want to kick up some dust both in the driver's seat and in their personal lives.[42] The Abarth/Sheen ad was viewed by audiences as more authentic and realistic than its predecessor, in which J. Lo drove a Fiat around the Bronx (viewers questioned whether J. Lo would drive anything in the Bronx these days, let alone a Fiat—and the commercial lost more credibility when discerning Bronxites realized it wasn't even filmed in New York). Sheen's ad, which highlighted his unhinged personality, might have been crazy, but it was real in a way that J. Lo's glammed-up, faux-homegirl spot wasn't. Fiat may have benefited from Sheen's bad behavior, but things only got worse for the actor. In 2015 he admitted to having HIV and paying millions in blackmail hush money over a four-year period to keep it a secret. Time will tell if Charlie's bad-boy image will continue to attract Madison Avenue and Hollywood, but shortly after making his revelations on the *Today* show, he was reportedly shopping his memoirs,[43] and he is now the new face of condom brand Lelo Hex.

My research shows that, depending on audience values, brand personality, and industry perception, audiences will more easily excuse certain social behaviors than others. Seventy-one percent of consumers will forgive an addiction, and 65 percent don't care about adultery. But 82 percent say they will not forgive racist attitudes, and 83 percent say that abusive behavior is unforgivable. So while we might overlook LaBeouf's bizarre conduct and chalk it up to child-star rebellion, it will be more difficult for an esteemed actor like Gary Oldman to overcome the damage of his anti-Semitic remarks[44]—it's unlikely that he'll secure another $12 million contract for Taiwanese mobile phone company HTC.

Every superstar partner comes with potential risk, but they also come with the opportunity for a big return. Millennials recognize the fakery of fame and value authenticity over a carefully crafted image. Instead of hoping and praying a celebrity has no skeletons in their closet (they almost always do), innovators, with the proper research, can cut through the image to a celebrity's true self, from controversial personal beliefs to triggers that can spark a breakdown (à la Britney Spears's umbrella attack in 2007). From there, you can develop a risk profile to determine whether that truth would negatively, or positively, affect brand perception.

I'm unapologetic not because I'm strong-willed or overconfident, I'm unapologetic because this is it; this is my life.

— JEAN SEBERG

After I named Michelle Obama one of the most influential fashion icons in *USA Today*, I was moved by the number of letters I received from black women thanking me for raising her profile as a style icon in the media. Black people have it rough in Hollywood. I remember how, during a casting session in Beverly Hills, a director described an A-list actress as being "pretty for a black girl"; he thought it was a compliment. I see how acting coaches in Los Angeles still assign the comedic or profoundly stupid character roles to their black students, under the guise of being "realistic." At movie premieres and after-parties and out and about in Hollywood, I'm disturbed by the number of black actors who feel they have no choice but to straighten their hair, bleach their skin, and butcher their noses in an attempt to westernize their look and dilute their identity; and it still doesn't get them what they want. And then there are those inspiring black women who have shown me the simple yet potent power of living the unapologetic life.

Black beauty company Carol's Daughter is the poster child for being fiercely, and unapologetically, who you are. Founder Lisa Price may have followed an unconventional route into the multibillion-dollar haircare industry in the early 1990s—she started out making all-natural body butters, oils, and fragrances in her Brooklyn kitchen and selling them at church flea markets—but the quality of her products soon caught on, and through word of mouth, Lisa found an audience among black women,[45] who spend far more on caring for their hair than any other demographic. Her devoted fan base grew as she added haircare products for black women who wore their hair naturally, like she did. "Good" hair has long been a loaded issue for black women, and those who refuse to conform to the white beauty standard of straight hair not only face pressure to defend their choice, especially in the workplace, but also have difficulty finding products that work for their hair's unique texture. Fans of the brand were so passionate that even black celebrities like Jada Pinkett Smith, Gabrielle Union, Mary J. Blige, and Oprah Winfrey spoke out about the products; the company's sales soon rocketed to $27 million.[46]

Carol's Daughter and its empress, Lisa Price, "got it": a company had finally arrived that understood the unique beauty needs of black women who had different skin, different hair, different features, and a very different definition of beauty than other women around the world. Black women are rarely portrayed as beautiful by the mainstream American media, which still heralds European ideals of beauty. Through its body oils and butters, Carol's Daughter believed that beauty came from within, giving a voice to those who had been overlooked and underappreciated for so long. Black fans and celebrities alike were excited to support an enterprise that was run by blacks, for blacks.

The brand soon started expanding into its own stores, as well as retailers like Target and Ulta, in addition to home shopping network giant HSN, and Carol's Daughter's beauty products and black-is-beautiful message entered the mainstream. By monitoring Facebook pages, black haircare blogs, and e-mails from customers, Lisa Price kept her finger on the pulse of her audience and continued to offer a highly tailored service. The company even created a special website for black women who were "transitioning" to natural hair—that is, protecting and growing out their once–chemically treated hair rather than cutting it all off and starting over.[47] When the company expanded into seven brick-and-mortar boutiques, customers could even get advice and demonstrations on how to use the products.

However, by 2011 sales began to plummet in the company's boutiques, and competitors like Miss Jessie's aggressively entered the natural hair market and sought share. Carol's Daughter began to struggle, and while Lisa Price still remained the face of the company, she ended up selling it to Pegasus Capital Advisors. In May 2014, Carol's Daughter stores filed for Chapter 11 bankruptcy protection.

Amid fans' fear that their favorite products would disappear, Carol's Daughter announced its new, lighter-skinned spokeswomen—Solange Knowles, Cassie, and Selita Ebanks— and a move toward "polyethnicity."[48] The backlash was immediate, and devotees of the brand questioned Lisa's commitment to championing black beauty. Blogger Honey Bii commented, " 'I'm not fair-complected . . . and by no means do I feel that [the ads] have to have this Afro-centric feel to it. But I feel like she sold us out.' "[49] While some recognized that the new campaign was as an attempt to cover more of the spectrum of black beauty, and that completely ignoring light-skinned women would be just as idiotic,[50] many black women who had helped birth the brand felt betrayed in favor of raking in cash from a broader demographic. Was Lisa Price, whose love for her black community, for her black identity, and for black economic prosperity was always as important as her products, selling out the very women who had emotionally and financially supported her rise to success?[51]

In 2014 Lisa Price posted a video announcement that quickly made the rounds on Facebook. In the video, Price expressed her excitement at the sale of Carol's Daughter to cosmetics giant L'Oréal. She spoke of how the global cosmetics company would take what she had built and solidify Carol's Daughter's place in history and beauty. She would continue to be the face of and creative force behind the company and head product development. For those fans who were in love with the all-black business, it was the final straw. "It's so sad black businesses don't see the value of staying on for the long haul," wrote one fan on the company's Facebook page.[52] In the minds of black women, L'Oréal was far from a minority-held company and had yet to prove its commitment to black beauty. Regardless, Lisa's announcement was undeniably confident and unapologetic: " 'We'll be operating as we have before, it'll be business as usual.' "[53] The new parent company brings Carol's Daughter the opportunity to have an even greater impact, reach international customers, and provide resources. Partnering with I AM THAT GIRL to create the #BORNANDMADE campaign—which encourages girls (and women) to unequivocally be who they are, regardless of what "anyone else" says[54]—indicates that the company is still true to its unapologetic roots, albeit with a little help from its new friend.

The Surprising Appeal of Kim Kardashian

You don't like me, fine, that's your prerogative.
But listen, I'm living my dream while you're
asleep wet-dreaming of it.

—KIM KARDASHIAN

Despite the enormous pressure to conform in Hollywood, Kim Kardashian never set out to fit in, and it's this exact nonconformity that drives our global obsession with her. Kim is a true game changer, redefining pre-established perceptions of what we consider to be beautiful, sexy, and successful. She has also pushed racial boundaries, not simply by marrying a black rapper but by pushing her family's way into the very "European" fashion and design world.[55] She's a new-school feminist, publishing an essay condemning slut shaming and, with her sisters, challenging the media's perception of what women's bodies are like (vaginas have gotten the silent treatment in the media, but in Kim's family vaginas bleed and push out babies just as those of billions of others do[56]). She has boldly championed some difficult causes: she made a documentary to bring awareness to mental health issues and participated in a PSA to reach victims of domestic violence. Kim is less interested in being accepted by others than by herself, and she hasn't taken the easier path of not thinking for herself and doing what everyone else is doing.

It wasn't until I was working on my Hollywood diversity study that I understood just how distinct Kim's fame was in a culture where white is right and everything else is not. A-listers often cover up their race and faith out of fear of losing the common vote, yet Kim remains unapologetically Armenian, championing her heritage and recently blasting the *Wall Street Journal* for running an ad that denied the mass killings of Armenians was genocide. She commemorates the 1915 event every year and has been welcomed in Armenia by its premier and heralded as putting the country on the map for millions. Compare this to the behavior of Muslim-born Zayn Malik and Gigi Hadid, or should I say Zain Javadd Malik and Jelena Noura Hadid. You would never know they were Muslim, as if it were a dirty little secret. But touting these exact types of differences will separate you from the pack and propel you to Kim Kardashian heights.

My research into the nature of Kim Kardashian's celebrity reveals that those who claim she is a Paris Hilton copycat actually rank Kim five times higher than most other celebrities on the characteristics of innovation versus imitation. Those who say she is nothing special, in truth, recognize her as being visually distinctive and differentiated among her peers. In fact, Kim's dark, exotic looks, ethnic features, and body shape are a far cry from the supposed beauty standards needed to resonate as a sex symbol in Hollywood. On a list of five hundred celebrities, Kim is rated as the least interchangeable or replaceable celebrity on the planet. This is no surprise. If you were to do a smash test on Kim Kardashian—pretend she's made of glass, pick her up and smash her on the floor—you'd still be able to recognize her from the broken pieces. However, if you did the same for Renée Zellweger, Reese Witherspoon, Jennifer Aniston, and others on the long list, you wouldn't be able to tell the difference. Among a sea of size triple-zero blondes, Kim has further amplified her distinctive looks and intense sexuality for power and wealth.

At the end of the day, Kim Kardashian is truly distinctive. She is a celebrity who has gained and retained our interest by consistently surprising us, not just with her naked antics but

CHAPTER 3

Expose

Tell the truth or someone will tell it for you.

—STEPHANIE KLEIN

*T*he news reports from Paris hit me as if I had been shot. I was six thousand miles away in Hollywood, glued to the TV and my phone, anxious for news of family and friends. Just days after the senseless slaughter of journalists at the offices of the French satirical weekly newspaper *Charlie Hebdo*, I was asked to represent a major film industry association and discuss Hollywood's pivotal role as a champion of the Je Suis Charlie movement, and what it meant for the future of free speech. I was honored by the invitation, but I had to decline. Je Suis Charlie was a slogan against censorship, a demand that all ideas be exposed to the same scrutiny and sunlight. Yet I knew that, in reality, this was the opposite of what Hollywood believed. This is an industry that regularly censors gays, scrubs out politics, and gives a stricter rating to films that feature a woman getting oral sex from a man than vice versa. I knew I'd get some blowback, but I just couldn't be part of Hollywood's attempt to claim the mantle of openness. If I really believed in Je Suis Charlie, I needed to stick to my guns. Je Suis Charlie = Je Suis Me.

Overexposure, to me, means being utterly connected with and open about what makes you, you. By overexposing yourself, your ideas, your products, and your services, you allow audiences unfiltered access to your true intentions—the how, what, and why of what you are doing. So, if you want to connect, take what you do best and own it. Be raw and honest. Be overexposed.

The Mysterious Case of Madame X

Out of your vulnerabilities will come your strength.

—SIGMUND FREUD

My next experience with France was a more pleasant one. In the spring of 2015, the Cannes Film Festival was well under way, and I was missing Europe and looking forward to getting a quick fix. On my way to the premiere of *Carol*, I noticed a strap slip from the shoulder of a well-known French actress who nervously scanned the room and then quickly pulled it back up. I wondered what she was hiding . . . and immediately thought of another Parisian with a strapless shoulder who got it right.

Virginie Amélie Avegno Gautreau was a white Creole born in New Orleans on January 29, 1859. After her father, a major in the Confederate army, was killed at the Battle of Shiloh, eight-year-old Amélie moved with her socially ambitious mother to Paris, where she was educated and introduced to high society. Before long she was celebrated for her striking looks and glamorous and exotic social presence. Amélie wasn't a conventional beauty, but her pale skin, flaming copper hair, sharp features, and exaggerated hourglass figure turned heads everywhere she went. Her charisma quickly won her a wealthy French banker husband, Pierre Gautreau. Women wanted to be her, while men wanted to sleep with her. Artists, not surprisingly, wanted to paint her.[1]

In 1884 an American painter named John Singer Sargent offered to paint Amélie's portrait for the stuffily bourgeois Paris Salon. He had one requirement—Amélie must be willing to expose her translucent skin, haughty demeanor, and raw sexuality in a highly provocative pose. Sargent instructed his muse to stand tall, proud, and brazen: her shoulders pulled back, her head cocked sharply to the left to emphasize her remarkable profile. He selected a long black satin skirt and a low-cut velvet bodice. Against the jet-black fabric, the deathly blue-white of her powdered skin is even more strange and striking. Amélie oddly turned her right arm so the underside was exposed as she gripped the top of a side table—an inviting and erotic gesture. Her left arm, in contrast, rests demurely on her hip. It is an unabashedly staged pose, which must have been challenging to hold even for a natural-born poser. During one sitting, Amélie's right shoulder strap dropped suggestively over her arm, and Sargent painted it that way.

When the painting, called *Madame X*, was exhibited in 1884, it unleashed pandemonium. Madame, one jeweled strap slipping off her shoulder, radiated a provocative and undeniable aura of sex, power, money, and disdain for the opinions of others. The matrons of Paris were appalled, yet nude paintings were commonplace in the Salon—Manet had exhibited his sublimely slutty *Olympia* in 1865[2]—so why was Amélie, certainly exposed but by no means naked, so scandalous? Perhaps it was the naked ambition and unabashed self-expression. Amélie was utterly overexposed and unapologetically self-centered: the heavy makeup, the overconfident pose, the *look* in her eyes. Women of social standing in nineteenth-century Paris simply didn't show that much.

Alas, Amélie had miscalculated the impact of her daring attitude. The portrait generated seismic controversy, but instead of catapulting Amélie into the highest levels of French society, it destroyed her. Once a social butterfly, she was reduced to being "escorted by municipal functionaries to the opera and other events." Sargent had to repaint the offending strap and return to London, unable to find work. Neither painter nor painted ever recovered from the scandal, and Amélie eventually disappeared from French society, supposedly removing all mirrors from her house and only leaving her home under cover of darkness.

Yet today, the power of overexposure to connect with audiences and elicit a response is undeniable. No one knows this better than Kim Kardashian. Like Amélie, Kim instinctively understands how to imbue objects with a symbolic weight infinitely more powerful than the objects themselves. Amélie had the misfortune to be born a hundred-plus years before her time; just imagine *her* on the cover of *Paper* magazine. Today, Madame X would be celebrated rather than shamed. Kim's object of symbolism is her iconic ass, whereas Amélie's symbolic object was her equally unforgettable shoulder. Kim's booty creates headlines not only because of its bounteous appearance, but because it's a forceful sign of her cultural power. Who else could have persuaded the most influential woman in fashion, Anna Wintour, to feature such unapologetic excess on the cover of *Vogue*?

One hundred fifty years later, Madame X lives on. Her iconic painting has evolved from shameful to seductive to aspirationally refined. Her fellow Real Housewives of La Rive Gauche—and their buttoned-up portraits—are long forgotten, while Amélie is immortal in her very brazenness.

YouTube #NoFilter

We're all going to die someday. Isn't it sad that you wasted your life being a terrible shit human being?

—Grace Helbig

My first job in Hollywood was at a celebrity PR firm in 2005, where I quickly learned that even the word *candid* wasn't what it seemed to be in showbiz. Those supposedly caught-in-the-act photos were actually heavily staged and made to look accidental. What they didn't yet know was that the real action was elsewhere. While Hollywood agents were obsessing over

Brad and Jen lookalikes—and busy covering up their secret lives—teenagers were making their own celebrities on YouTube. These stars' very source of power was that they had no filters and didn't cover anything up. They were *real*. Nine years later in 2014, I published my study on YouTube stars in *Variety* and declared that the new breed of celebrity had arrived. I found myself in the midst of a global media frenzy, fending off book deals, speaking engagements, and board seat offers. I certainly didn't expect that. My research on YouTube stars certainly confirmed for me that they were the next big thing, but most importantly, through it I've learned the sheer power of being off script and on point.

YouTube's stars, most famously PewDiePie (who has over 47 million subscribers),[3] reach more people more frequently and more intimately than any established Hollywood star. PewDiePie's net worth is $61 million, 625 times more than the net worth of the average American household.[4] Even lesser known YouTubers, like Brazilian comedian HolaSoyGerman, are making serious bank by fully committing to hare-brained stunts, gross-out comedy, or foulmouthed speech. In a curious reversal of traditional celebrity, the bigger the YouTube star, the more willing they are to both physically and emotionally overexpose themselves.

This new breed of celebrity has phenomenal influence on Millennials and their younger siblings. Fans find them more relatable than Hollywood celebrities, who they perceive as aloof and manufactured. These digital superstars have quickly captured the hearts and minds of their fans and represent enormous opportunity for both Hollywood and Madison Avenue.

While mainstream celebrities may think they are already baring it all—Gwen Stefani chats about her split from cheating-with-the-nanny husband Gavin Rossdale ("I thought it was over for me . . . I think the hardest thing I did was to get out of bed and go to the studio")[5] and Lady Gaga shows literally everything by taking off her clothes for Tom Ford—their audiences, even sympathetic ones, perceive only highly curated and contrived transparency. Having grown up with so-called reality TV, Millennials and Gen Zers are well aware that "real" situations are often set up for desired results, cast for particular clashes of personality, and edited for drama and pathos. Notorious yo-yo dieter Oprah Winfrey's "heartfelt" confession of her "food addiction" and partnership with Weight Watchers has many rolling their eyes with skepticism: "It doesn't change anything. She isn't a registered/licensed PhD dietician with some new secret. She is a marketing juggernaut that will sell processed sludge to adoring millions. Hype-de-doodly doo."[6] Only in this case she didn't sell anything, and shares fell 61 percent since the announcement that Oprah would join the board. When Jemima Kirke of *Girls* made a video on the importance of women sharing their stories of having abortions, commenters made it clear that "the sincerity [she] is trying to convey doesn't quite come across. Her attempt at being approachable and concerned is an overt veneer."[7]

Today, ideas and individuals alike have to bare their true selves. Jenna Marbles has made a one-woman empire out of talking about her "before" looks and the hard work it takes to get them to a socially acceptable "after" state. Her "How to Trick People into Thinking You're Good Looking" video[8] currently has 65 million views (imagine James Franco or Johnny Depp doing that). Onision, aka YouTube's Perfect Villain, posts his wildly controversial views on anything from rape to depression and is best known for his inane "I'm a Banana" song, which earned 40 million views and a mention as "Video of the Week" on Comedy Central's web-soup series *Tosh.0*. YouTube stars are also literally accessible, and as fans bond with their cyberspace heroes, they develop far stronger loyalty than they feel for traditional, untouchable celebrities. This loyalty remains unshakable as long as their expectations are met.[9] Look at the comment threads on videos such as "I Hate Joey Graceffa,"[10] where fans and stars face off over a barrage of insults. Gamer and comedian KSI took it as far as making a video of himself responding to viewers responding to his videos.[11] This is the level of openness the market demands today, and those that seek to connect with their audiences need to follow these cyberstars' lead and bare their souls as well as their bodies.

Just because I deliver the message offensively doesn't mean I'm not right.

— ONISION

Nearly seven in ten young people describe their relationships with YouTube celebrities as intimate and personal. Intimacy is everything, yet some of the traditional moves in the Hollywood playbook are actually adding distance between stars and fans. YouTube celebrities' lack of presence on both the big screen and magazine covers seems to *add* to their overall appeal and credibility.

Hollywood celebrities who have gotten used to trading on their sex appeal need to watch out. Most YouTube stars may not fit the heralded Midwestern Hollywood look, but this no longer matters to younger audiences. In fact, YouTube celebrities and traditional celebrities are considered to be equally attractive because Millennials and Generation Zers redefine celebrity desirability in a more diverse and multidimensional manner. Cookie-cutter pretty girls and boys next door are being overrun by those with more unique looks, and goddess-like curves are less important than the humor, warmth, and imagination that give YouTube stars the edge. Today's fans are more likely to be engaged and excited by someone who can make them laugh and inspire empathy—and if they happen to be hot, well, that's gravy.

So what can ideas, products, services, and traditional celebrities learn from all of this? The key is to understand how all these different factors add up. YouTube stars like Markiplier and PrankvsPrank connect because they reflect the things Millennials and Gen Zers find important. These digital icons are seen as 90 percent more genuine than "traditional" celebrities. Teens love that they show more of their personality quirks (or even flaws) and seem "realer" than celebs who've broken through in more traditional ways: 88 percent of young people agree that big-screen stars are "faker" than YouTube celebrities. Most teens do not see a boundary between a YouTube celebrity's work and life. In contrast, they perceive traditional celebs as behaving one way at work and being something else in real life. All this adds up to a YouTuber being far more likely to influence a fan to make a purchase.

In early 2016, YouTube A-listers the Fine Bros took a misstep in attempting to monetize their "React" format and trademark the word *React*.[12] The duo had established their dominance over the reaction video format—a series of videos in which they filmed themselves reacting to other videos. They sought to capitalize on the opportunity by creating a template that would allow users to upload their own videos directly under the Fines' React banner. Longtime fans went ballistic, believing, incorrectly, that the Fines now owned the whole concept of reaction videos and would be legally entitled to ban fan-made reaction videos. Far from being embraced as a new-world, online Hollywood studio, the Fines were

forced to back away from their bold plan, irreparably harm-
ing their relationship with their fan base. YouTube stars who
have attempted to cross over into Hollywood, such as comedy
duo Smosh, have been heavily penalized by their fans who re-
sent this compromising of the anticelebrity ethos.[13] Fans are fine
with YouTube superstars becoming millionaires off their videos
alone, but they will never forgive having their relationship ex-
ploited for a quick dollar through old-school celebrity tactics.

Beauty and the Biotech

The truth is more heroic than the hype.

— JESSICA LYNCH

Nearly a year after the global frenzy around my YouTube star
declaration had died down, I was ready for my next challenge.
I had recently been paying closer attention to the world of
start-ups, and how technology CEOs were marketing themselves as the celebrities of Silicon Valley. I knew I had to head
to San Francisco, and it was there that I encountered Biotech
Barbie—otherwise known as Elizabeth Holmes, founder of
the controversial startup Theranos, Inc.

When Holmes appeared on the cover of *Fortune* magazine
at the age of thirty, Theranos became the biggest and most
promising biotech company no one had ever heard of. Elizabeth founded her company when she was nineteen, and eleven
years later she had created a revolutionary blood-testing de-
vice that could conduct dozens of tests with a single finger
prick and a drop of blood. It was as sexy as the diagnostic-lab
industry was going to get, and media and medics alike fell
head over heels in love. Theranos boasted a swanky board of

directors, including former U.S. secretaries of state Henry Kissinger and George P. Schultz and former U.S. senators Sam Nunn and William H. Frist. The lab raised over $800 million from investors and was soon valued at a staggering $9 billion. Elizabeth was hailed as the world's youngest self-made paper billionaire, was celebrated for shaking up the healthcare industry, and seemingly overnight became the new face of techpreneurship.

Her rags-to-riches story reminded many of the Horatio Alger myth: a young unknown from an undistinguished background—she dropped out of Stanford at the age of nineteen—makes good through sheer hard work and determination. Elizabeth took Alger's American hero one step further with the humanitarianism of her vision. "At a relatively early age I began to believe that building a business was perhaps the greatest opportunity for making an impact," she said, "because it's a tool for making a change in the world."[14]

Elizabeth's success story began with her uncle's fight with cancer. Patients often aren't diagnosed with an illness until they show symptoms, which can be too late to provide lifesaving treatment. Elizabeth wanted to provide people with a cheaper and faster way to detect their health risks, giving them in turn an earlier opportunity to seek treatment and make lifestyle changes to improve their health.[15] Theranos promised exactly that by transferring control of blood work from physicians and insurance companies to the patient. For roughly $7, anyone could walk into Walgreens—without a prescription—and order blood work. Results were quick, confidential, and delivered straight to your inbox with no doctor's visit required. Instead of vials of blood, the company heralded its one-drop "Nanotainer" as a cheap, fast, and painless alternative.

Elizabeth was a triple threat: incredibly smart, staggeringly ambitious, and easy on the eyes. She cut a memorable figure in public with her black turtleneck and blond chignon. She clearly enjoyed the media attention, reveling in her own cover stories and close-ups.

Yet Theranos was a company shrouded in silence. Holmes and her fellow board members had always remained tight-lipped about the effectiveness of the technology and the inner workings of the start-up, citing trade secrets. As the company grew, there was increasing pressure to explain exactly how the proprietary technology could "perform hundreds of tests, from standard to sophisticated, from a pinprick and tiny sample of blood"[16] given that no one had ever come close to such a feat before. While Elizabeth continued to use jargon like "optimizing the chemistry" and "leveraging software" to evade questions, audiences became increasingly suspicious. Journalists began to observe that her "body language [was that] of someone who is fiercely protective and on guard"[17] (and the ever-present black turtleneck probably didn't help). One interviewer noted, "Talking to Holmes is a bit like talking to a politician—she's politely impenetrable, unspooling a stream of words without actually revealing very much."[18]

Meanwhile, Holmes's corporate alter ego wasn't faring much better. On October 16, 2015, the *Wall Street Journal* revealed the significant cracks in the glossy veneer of Theranos in a blockbuster front-page exposé. The company had such little faith in its own technology that it was outsourcing some of its $7 blood tests to traditional blood-testing labs that billed the company as much as $300 to process the tests. In November 2016 the Centers for Medicare and Medicaid Services (CMS) dropped by Theranos's Newark, California, laboratory. What they found was startling. "It was determined that the deficient practices of the laboratory pose immediate jeopardy to patient health and safety," stated a follow-up ultimatum sent to Theranos on January 25, 2016.[19] Theranos had ten days to comply with vital hematology-related and other lab requirements. Walgreens immediately stopped all testing in its Palo Alto, California, locations and ordered Theranos to process all blood tests from the drug retailer's locations at its Arizona lab.

Instead of laying herself bare and opening up about the company's inner workings, Elizabeth doubled down. The company actively avoided peer review, seeking out less-probing technology and finance media coverage rather than offering specific details of its research and methodology to medical journals. Stanford School of Medicine professor John Ioannidis accused Theranos of "stealth research,"[20] and even the once-adoring tech execs[21] and bloggers who experienced the so-called revolutionary technology wrote about getting blood work results from the start-up that contradicted results from their own doctors.[22]

Holmes's attempts at damage control after the *Wall Street Journal* exposé appeared calculating and contrived. During a tech conference panel (organized, ironically, by the *WSJ*) she insisted that Theranos was "completely transparent" about its procedures and data, yet she failed to address any of the major concerns that had been highlighted. When she boldly claimed that the *WSJ*'s anonymous sources were "clearly very confused," it smacked of protesting too much. And when she promised "a very long document about to go on the Internet" that would explain everything,[23] Holmes came across as defensive rather than open to admitting and addressing mistakes. Both Theranos and Holmes, though outwardly claiming transparency, were embodying its opposite.

Overexposure goes beyond surface image. Your pitch may get you noticed, but it's the honesty and humanity of your idea that will ensure you reach and connect with today's audiences, who demand unprecedented openness. When initial claims against Theranos were raised, Elizabeth boldly denied them, but as the negative reports multiplied, she faded into the background and issued a declarative statement on the company's website. Theranos became the poster child for false transparency and tech-bubble charlatanism. While it sought a starring role in the healthcare industry, where maximum exposure is essential, its substance was hype and hyperbole.

For the already overexposed, in contrast, the *Wall Street Journal* poses no such threat. Had Elizabeth Holmes been forthright about her company's goals and challenges, her daring attitude might well have propelled her somewhere other than disaster. Instead, under the guise of overexposure, she boldly promoted style over substance and strategically shielded her company's practices and products from full industry scrutiny. Ultimately, Elizabeth hid behind digital disclaimers and shunned the very media she had once aggressively courted. She promised to set the world on fire with Theranos, but instead her overreach started a fire in her own start-up.

The Panini, the Pedophile, and the Pimp

If there's one thing that Hollywood has taught me it's that sex sells, especially if done in an overexposed way, but I've also learned that it's not a good idea to serve it with your favorite sandwich. Subway found this out the hard way. In 1998 Jared Fogle was a 425-pound college student ashamed of his body, unpopular with girls, ostracized by his peers, and very lonely. When the fat around his neck started choking him in his sleep, Fogle realized he needed to make a change.[24] Jared dropped 245 pounds, over half his body weight,[25] and the rest, as they say, is history. Fifteen years later, the Subway spokesman was making a killing, promoting his tale of turkey sandwiches everywhere from *Dr. Phil* to troop bases in the Middle East. Other Subway spokespeople with stronger star power, such as Olympian Michael Phelps,[26] came and went, but it was Jared's everyman tale of beating his bulge with six-inch sandwiches that created the most buzz.

After fifteen years of working with Jared, Tony Pace, the CMO of Subway, acknowledged that while Fogle was "a bit hokey," he was "family" and "woven into the fabric of the brand."[27] Even after a widely reported gain of forty pounds, Subway stood by Jared and praised the "length and authenticity of Jared's endorsement as a real person who, despite his struggles, has maintained a healthy lifestyle by eating Subway.' "[28]

But perhaps Tony spoke too soon. Suddenly, *Dr. Phil* had a new Jared-related story to tell. In the spring of 2015 an undercover FBI operation exposed Jared's double life, revealing that he had in fact traded his food addiction for a sex addiction, with six-year-olds. Hundreds of photos and videos of child pornography were recovered from his computer. It was a difficult story to digest. The all-star American weight-loss champ was a bona fide pedophile. For a brief moment it looked like Jared might escape criminal charges by putting the blame on someone else: Russell Taylor, the manager of his charity, the Jared Foundation, was charged with child exploitation, possession of child pornography, and voyeurism.[29] Then a "friend" turned on Jared and released tapes of him fantasizing about sex with underage girls and boys.[30] Jared's career as fast-food pitchman was officially over, as was his marriage, his image, and just about everything else in his life.

Around the same time that Fogle, and by extension Subway, was fumbling at the crucial moment of the game, a Hooter's-waitress-turned-hooker (and freelance pimp) named Aziah King, better known as Zola, openly tweeted about her "hoe-ism" on a trip to Florida. Her 142-tweet, breathtaking story of stripping, prostitution, kidnapping, murder, and attempted suicide captivated the internet and skyrocketed Zola to stardom. Zola claimed she traveled with a girl named Jessica to dance at strip clubs in Florida but instead ended up pimping out Jessica. Zola proudly told of advising Jess that "pussy is worth thousands." Her Twitter epic included tales of watching Jess banging a pimp known as Z in front of her boyfriend, Jarrett; witnessing Jess being kidnapped by another pimp (who was eventually shot in the face); and seeing Jarrett jump off the hotel balcony in protest over Jessica prostituting herself— only to be saved by his pants catching on something and leaving him dangling four stories high. Zola then claimed to have received a phone call from Jess in jail a few days later after being arrested for prostitution, along with Z, who was wanted for kidnapping and murder charges. Zola returned to Twitter to prove to haters that she wasn't lying about the Twitter tale and to post updates on Jessica (including photos of her former friend, now pregnant and with a new man).[31]

Zola's tweets were crazy, sexy, and cool, but they also veered into a new realm of criminal behavior and sexual abuse. A *Washington Post* investigation revealed that her companions, Jessica and Z, had played this hustle before, luring another desperate young woman into "trapping" against her will.[32] Zola's unhinged overexposure—seemingly too crazy to be true— actually told an only slightly exaggerated story. By going way, way beyond transparency and fully exposing every detail of who, what, how, and why, Zola forced a conversation that most of us don't want to have—namely, how young people (girls in this case, but equally boys) are vulnerable to predators who know how to fit in, appease parents and partners, and say the right things to get what they want.

Zola is the antithesis of Fogle. While Jared apparently opened up about his weight loss to the world, he was in fact hiding his far darker true nature. Zola, on the other hand,

overexposed herself by discussing her philosophy on prostitution and vibing on her hoeism. If Subway had taken a cue from
Zola, it would have used the power of exposure to connect
with audiences who not only respect but are also captivated by
the unadulterated truth. Rather than covering up, denying
responsibility, and trying to make the problem go away, Subway could have used the moment to open up a national conversation about vulnerable children. Instead, the company
issued a brief statement in the hope of quickly distancing the
brand from the debacle, as if Jared had never existed, and the
millions of people who had followed his story for fifteen years
would just forget. Instead of sweeping something so serious
under the rug, the sandwich chain could have shown it was
hurting. After all, as Tony Pace put it, Jared was family.

Jared's demise was not only a PR disaster for the organization but also a reason to question the morals, ethics, and credibility of several Subway employees. This became apparent after
rumors circulated that the chain knew about Jared's "prefer-
ences" as early as 2008.[33] Jared's exposure could have been a true
milestone in the organization's life; everyone from the CEO
down could have spoken out. What could have been more compelling than stories, tweets, and posts from employees who had
firsthand experience with a pedophile? Subway would become
known as a crusader for public justice, committed to the fight
against pedophilia. The brand would have transitioned from
a sandwich shop to an icon of corporate heroism. But now,
Subway's DNA will forever remain connected to pedophilia—
in a negatively opaque, not a positively exposed, way.

Zola and Subway have both moved on, the latter to a
marketing challenge where its number-one asset is now its
number-one liability, the former to a life filled with potential
movie, book, and product opportunities. People who operate

within old paradigms, hiding their real feelings about their uncomfortable truths, are missing a valuable opportunity to forge a truly compelling connection with their audiences.

Keeping It Real

> People often tell me to smile . . . It got me thinking, do I have resting bitch face?
>
> —ME

I was racing from taping my interview for *The Insider* to meet a producer for dinner at SoHo House in West Hollywood. Ariana Grande had been caught on camera licking a donut and claiming she hated America, and everyone was asking me if the pop princess was finito. At dinner, I couldn't help but get distracted by the real Real Housewives on a "girls' night out" sitting at the table next to us. These women were masterpieces. Their faces were taut, their veneers white, and their bodies tight. Yet despite having invested all this time and energy into looking hot, something wasn't quite right. While they had acquired a sexy look, they weren't quite exuding a sexy vibe. In fact, they seemed rather asexual, and I couldn't help but wonder when they had last gotten laid. We've all become experts at seeing beyond the façade, me included. I learned that to really create a believable image what you show on the outside has to match what you feel on the inside.

The buzzword phrase *resting bitch face* has been around since the mid-2000s,[34] although it really came to fame in 2013 thanks to thousands of internet memes and a breakout YouTube video by funny guys Broken People.[35] The likes of Natalie Portman,

Karl Lagerfeld, and even HM Queen Elizabeth II became poster bitches for the term, and tabloids had a field day naming and shaming the top resting bitch faces across the nation. Some claimed the phrase itself was inherently sexiest, oblivious to the fact that men can be some of the biggest bitches around. For those who missed out on the mania, resting bitch face is an attempt at a neutral facial expression to hide what you're really thinking and feeling. Think of Kristen Stewart's disengaged red-carpet stare, Anna Wintour's Ice Queen demeanor, or Kanye West's blank look as he pushes his way through the paps. The problem is that most people walk away with the perception that the person is showing a hint of disdain.

What Kanye, Kristen, and other celebs, like the notoriously resting-bitch-faced Anna Kendrick, who demonstrated hers on *The Late Late Show with James Corden*,[36] don't yet realize is that the days of poker face are over. Unless you're Her Majesty the Queen, a blank face—cum—bitchy expression no longer earns you respect or buys you a break. These days, audiences can see through the veneer of neutrality and are demanding overexposure instead. What's true for celebs is true for ideas, products, and services: if you want to connect, you have to be overexposed. If you say one thing, but feel another, Millennials and Gen Zers will rarely forgive you for your deception. Companies and leaders can learn from reactions to resting bitch face, because it reveals just how intuitively their audiences can suss out real emotions, feelings, and beliefs behind the fake ones.

Most empathetic humans are able to the detect emotional cues in a resting bitch face. A recent study suggests that the strongest emotion seen in most is contempt.[37] Feeling contemptuous isn't the problem, but *hiding* the fact that you are feeling contempt is. We suspect that Simon Cowell is secretly disapproving of his fellow judges and the *X-Factor* no-hopers he spends his days critiquing—and this suspicion is backed up by the work of researchers at Noldus Information Technology, who ran celeb candid shots (including Cowell's) through a facial analysis system. Five hundred points on the face were analyzed to assign an expression of either happiness, sadness, anger, fear, surprise, disgust, contempt, or neutrality.[38] They found that while genuinely neutral expressions might have a touch of sadness or a hint of kindness, those with resting bitch face overwhelmingly were hiding contempt in their blank looks. This contempt—revealed by "one side of the mouth pulled back slightly, the eyes squinting a little," or a tightening around the eyes and slightly raised corners of the mouth, is subtle but unmistakable.[39] And, in the age of overexposure, hiding the ugly truth of what you really feel is the biggest mistake anyone can make.

Ideas and enterprises that try to disguise what they really believe behind a façade of politeness or helpfulness miss out on an even deeper level of connection with consumers. Tired of being hated, Coca-Cola continues to tap-dance around the issue that they make money by selling liquid sugar with campaigns that promote sharing and caring (ideas usually sold to preschool viewers of *Sesame Street*). Whether it's "personalized" bottles that invite you to share a Coke with "Rob" or "a rock star" or commercials that show the company's concerned efforts to help in the war against obesity, Coca-Cola should reconsider its "mission" to "refresh the world . . . to inspire moments of happiness . . . to create value and make a difference."[40]

This approach is creating ideas that are generating significant backlash. The Center for Science in the Public Interest used "Coke's custom label generator, a tool that lets you tag a bottle with whatever names you want to see in the soda brand's iconic lettering" to share a Coke with Obesity.[41] Coke's attempt to reposition its image with a commercial touting its responsible actions, including putting calorie counts on labels, removing sugary drinks from schools, and offering more low-cal/no-cal drinks was ridiculed by a remake that used the same video with a new voiceover listing the health dangers of diet soda.[42]

What resting bitch face teaches us is that you need to be relentless about sharing your true thoughts and feelings. Forget resting bitch face—if you want to connect and engage with your product, service, or ideas, you need to adopt the attitude of an Active Bitch Face instead. Instead of applying a veneer of neutrality over your feelings or "positioning" your ideas, Active Bitch Face is all about exposing what you truly think and feel in a completely raw and utterly candid way. Look at a brand like Mountain Dew, whose 2016 Super Bowl spot was the utterly bonkers #puppymonkeybaby.[43] This disturbing CGI creation perfectly exposes the brand's deranged DNA. The #puppymonkeybaby is creepy, hilarious, and absurd, but it's also completely authentic. Many Super Bowl viewers found it nauseating, but the product's fans loved it. Mountain Dew is the perfect example of a brand that is more than happy to overexpose itself, all the time.

Similarly, Chick-fil-A stays true to its ultra-conservative Christian beliefs and closes on Sundays, keeps Christmas in its holiday advertising, and donates to anti-gay causes. An initial pledge to stay out of politics and decrease anti-gay giving seems to have been short-lived.[44] Despite boycotts and protests staged by equal rights supporters, Chick-fil-A continues to pray and profit. Sales reached $5.8 billion in 2014 and exceeded those of fast-food chains with twice as many locations.[45] Chick-fil-A is more than happy to show its true self, all the time—its fans remain determined to follow the spokes-cow's advice to "Eat mor chikin." All products, ideas, and services need to be just as relentlessly self-expressed and overexposed.

The Science of Exposure

> The point of vulnerability is a relinquishing of control, not a tool for further control.
>
> —MARK MANSON

Believe it or not, there was a time when Kim Kardashian dreamed of becoming a teacher at Marymount High School, Kris Kardashian was simply Nicole Brown Simpson's bestie, and Caitlyn was just a twinkle in Bruce Jenner's eye. Back then Madonna did a pretty good job of being the world's most over-exposed provocateur. When I was sixteen, Madge released her encyclopedia of high-style shagging, *Sex*. Co-starring Naomi Campbell, Isabella Rossellini, Vanilla Ice, and other half-life celebrities from the NYC club world, *Sex* was—predictably—denounced as degrading by everyone from the Catholic Church (Madge's home team) to antiporn feminists *and* sex-positive writers. Even *Rolling Stone* found Madonna's musings about anal sex, cunnilingus, blow jobs, and bondage more laughable than sexy. No one seemed to like it, but it hardly mattered, since no one could buy it either—the coffee table book, bound with an aluminum cover and sealed in Mylar plastic, sold out its entire print run just days after it was released.

Madonna intuitively understood that if your critics hate you for showing too much, then show them even more. And by the looks on her face, the self-proclaimed "Queen of Pop" loved every moment. In fact, research has since proven what Madonna and now Kim, with her penchant for posting nude selfies, instinctively know: overexposure is exciting and exhilarating. If you want to understand why today's biggest celebrities and brands should be quick to share every thought—from the banal to the crazy to the brilliant—just look at the science.

Despite what the Old Testament says, there is nothing inherently humble about *Homo sapiens*. Human beings are programmed to think about themselves and to enjoy sharing their self-obsession with the world. A scientific study has shown that we find talking about ourselves more rewarding than earning a small sum of money for keeping quiet. Those few minutes of indulgence are literally and biochemically blissful. They fire up the same dopamine-drenched neural pathways as do drugs, food, and sex. We also use 30 to 40 percent of our speech to talk about our subjective experiences of the world ("I think, I want, I feel"), and 80 percent of our social media posts share our own immediate experiences and emotional relationships.

The need to express ourselves kicks in at an early age. Unlike other primates, human babies begin to share their experiences of the world at around nine months. In fact, the urge to share is so strong that the same study has suggested that being allowed to express our opinions about the world is a subjective reward—something that both feels good and is socially encouraged.[46]

The end result is that all humans find it highly rewarding to be self-referential *and* have the opportunity to share those thoughts with other people, so much so that overexposure becomes its own reward. It creates an evolutionary advantage by strengthening social bonds. Even gossip has an evolutionary function—by sharing learned information rather than having to learn it ourselves firsthand, we exponentially accelerate the amount of information we can absorb in a lifetime and help each other make good decisions about who to trust, among other things.

There's a caveat, of course. Overexposure and authenticity are linked—exposing a false version of ourselves to the world just doesn't feel as good, no matter how much attention we get. Just like the 2000s hit parade of born-again Disney pop virgins who eventually derailed into a more authentic life of crack cocaine and rehab, there's nothing pleasurable about pretending to be a nicer—or "better"—person than you really are. Overexposure only works when it's the real deal, and this best plays out on social media, where the more real you are, the more approval you receive, creating a positive cycle. Users with high self-esteem benefit more from exposing themselves than do their more self-conscious friends. People with lower self-esteem get correspondingly lower levels of feedback on their more modest posts. As they experience fewer rewarding reactions, they in turn are less and less likely to post intimate, revealing, and "real" status updates about themselves—further decreasing the feel-good factor that overexposure offers.[47]

So, those who are truly self-obsessed and willing to overexpose their real selves around the clock get three big rewards for their behavior: they are able to fully express their true selves and feel good about it, gain widespread yet also intimate attention, and carve out a distinct place for themselves where this attention and self-expression can increase their popularity. Overexposure is a zero-sum game; you have to be fully committed in order to reap its rewards.

In the fall of 2014, Madonna took to Instagram to beg listeners not to listen to the leaked demos for her *Rebel Heart* album—exactly the opposite of what she should have done.[48]

If you want to connect, you have to expose everything: flaws, flat notes, unsynced tempos, and all. If only Madonna had learned something from Kim Kardashian, who overexposes herself all the time. After Kim was inundated with hate for posting yet another not-safe-for-work selfie, she called out some of her more famous critics on Twitter for their hypocrisy rather than trying to cover up the controversy. Kim followed up by posting an essay on her own empowerment in honor of International Women's Day: "I am empowered by my body. I am empowered by my sexuality. I am empowered by feeling comfortable in my skin. I am empowered by showing the world my flaws and not being afraid of what anyone is going to say about me."[49] And this is the secret of overexposure—it transcends narcissism or self-obsession. Overexposing ourselves is in fact a powerfully connective tool. When we overexpose our thoughts, feelings, and ideas, we empower ourselves to tell a much bigger and more honest story than we do when we try to control how people think, feel, and respond to our work.

> I'm never one to preach, but I felt really positive and really good about myself. I love the photos, I did it for me, I hope other people like them.
>
> —KIM KARDASHIAN

The world was first overexposed to Kim Kardashian in 2007, when *Kim K Superstar*, also starring R&B singer Ray J, was released by Vivid Entertainment. The thirty-nine-minute video became the best-selling sex tape of all time. Kim denied she leaked the tape: "I'm not poor. I'm not desperate. . . . It's something I feel betrayed by."[50] Regardless of whether she was, in fact, taken advantage of by others, Kim's comfort in her own skin was abundantly clear even back then. She has since bared all for *Playboy* and *Paper* magazine, not to mention a myriad of selfies in between.

So what differentiates Kim's naked pics from those of a sea of other celebrities who have also stripped for Instagram? The difference is twofold. First, Kim has full ownership and control of her photographs. No one exposes Kim but Kim: "I think there's power in that and I think I have the control to put out what I want so even if I'm objectifying myself, I feel good about it."[51] Second, they *are* Kim, and have become an inherent part of her brand's DNA. She posts her nude selfies openly and responds to both her critics and fans unashamedly. When Bette Midler trolled Kim on Twitter and slammed her NSFW selfie, Kim called her out on it; in the same Twitter chain, she flirted with fans who loved it. The coup de grâce came when she followed up with yet another nude pic, "#Liberated."

My research into the nature of Kim Kardashian's celebrity reveals that those who insist her rise to fame was only because of her sex tape also say it's not possible to become famous (or stay famous) by releasing a sex tape. Incidentally, those who entirely pin Kim's success on a sex tape are twice as likely to want to make one themselves. Those who label Kim Kardashian a "slut" also claim to admire strong women who are proud of showing their bodies. Over 72 percent agree that women have the right to use their femininity and sexuality to their advantage. In fact, most people would be more likely to dress provocatively if they felt better about their bodies.

Kim Kardashian resonates with today's audiences not only because she's fearless but also because she is honest and unashamed. She is utterly connected and open about who she is, and she allows you to see through to her intention—regardless of whether you like it or not. Kim is overexposed. You didn't like the fact that she made $5 million on her sex tape? It doesn't matter, because she liked it. "I think I definitely over share, but I'm really engaged."[52] Audiences respond to this exact vulnerability, candidness, type of storytelling, and lack of façade. Like Kim, ideas, products, and services that overexpose themselves and reveal their true intentions will break through and find their own fans.

CHAPTER 4

Lead

You don't have to like me,
I'm not a Facebook status.

—Wiz Khalifa

"*I* can fuck anyone I want, so don't fuck with me." With that I learned that nothing in Hollywood is simple, especially sex. It was the morning my friend Christian, a powerful porn executive, invited me to his studio in the porn capital of the world, the San Fernando Valley, just a short drive from Hollywood. That's when I first witnessed gay for pay in action, when the ripped guy I recognized as the devoted husband (with two kids) from my gym walked onto the set, naked, and nonchalantly took his position ready for his cock-in-ass close-up. I later learned that the actor, Sebastian, was in fact straight off camera, but saw no conflict in getting paid to be gay for the cameras. I was suddenly, newly resolved to define myself and not let others define me.

By similarly refusing to be labeled as one thing or another, our most significant business leaders are also our biggest superstars. Whether it's Steve Jobs unveiling Apple's latest iPhone or supermodel-turned-CEO Tyra Banks terrifying her wannabe models, leaders have to have rock star charisma. Leadership, at least in the business world, was once about buttoning up—not showboating. Your job was to set a vision and align people with it. However, thanks to the likes of Virgin's Richard Branson, SpaceX's Elon Musk, and Yahoo's Marissa Mayer, there's now no shame in CEOs seeking the spotlight. These leaders are as close to their publicists as they are to their colleagues in the C-suite. As a result, star quality has become a requirement for leadership appeal. At the same time, celebrities are expanding their roles to become businesspeople. Jessica Alba is a Golden Globe nominee and the founder of The Honest Company; Diddy spends less time singing than producing Sean John clothing and wrangling employees at Revolt TV; Dr. Dre hit the big time (again) with Beats; and Posh Spice became designer extraordinaire Victoria Beckham. The list of savvy stars who are quick to capitalize on the new face of leadership is exploding.

And, of course, pop culture and politics are linked, as our politicians are bona fide superstars. Barack Obama has the effortless black boy cool of Denzel Washington, while Donald Trump embodies the extreme self-obsession of Marlon Brando. Even our ultra-villains, like ISIS's beheading video star Jihadi John or Vladimir Putin, know how to stage a scene, play to the cameras, and excite their audiences. So, what does this mean for those who want to create sharable content and culture-shifting business ideas? How can we become leaders who take the world by storm?

The Lessons of Leadership

A strong spirit transcends rules.

— PRINCE

Seeing the way leadership works in the real world is a tad more enlightening than reading case studies as an MBA student at Harvard Business School. Millions wonder how a bankrupt businessman with a tanking reality TV show became president of the United States. How is it that a French shoemaker manages to convince the modern woman that there is no panache without excruciating pain? Why do predictable pop stars like Taylor Swift and Ariana Grande create fan frenzies? If you want to create breakthrough ideas, you need to understand the people and ideas that are, in fact, breaking through and accept the realities of why they are resonating.

These polarizing personalities know exactly what they want, when they want it, how they like it, and most importantly they are not afraid to show it. Like celebrities, successful business leaders today make their agenda personal, often dominate the boardroom, and nearly always look good while they're doing it. Not only do they ignore "rules" and "expectations," they roll right over them. It's this inner passion, conviction, and refusal to fit neatly in a box that has redefined the world's can-do attitude and creates a real connection with today's audiences. The stakes are high, and the only way to connect with Millennials is to show them that your passion—whether for technology, medical innovation, or spreading mayhem—is real and unstoppable.

Leaders and the breakthrough ideas they generate have less to do with old-school notions of consensus, collaboration, and considered reasoning and more to do with getting "things done in complex, interdependent systems in which people pursue multiple, often conflicting, agendas"[1]—aka whatever you need to do in order to do exactly what you think is right. In doing so, you hit the mark by striking an emotional nerve with audiences.

Consider the fast-talking and "straight-shooting" Donald Trump. Despite his "xenophobia and arrogance on immigration and foreign policy . . . there's also another reason he continued to sit atop the Republican polls: he speaks a particular kind of truth about some issues the way only someone with no filter can."[2] Then there's his onetime opponent Jeb Bush, who's been described as so "mind-numbingly unoriginal [he] can't even express those unoriginal ideas in a politically adept manner."[3] Trump declares his beliefs loud and proud, political correctness be damned. No one can remain neutral—you either love him because he's a groundbreaker or hate him because of his "gutter politics."[4] Does anyone even remember what Jeb had to say, let alone care about it? What about the Democratic "good wife" Hillary Clinton, who was the current poster child for secrecy and being chased by the FBI for deleting 31,380 potentially classified e-mails?

Just as Trump and Clinton needed to win at all costs, balancing being "real" with confronting barriers that prevent them from connecting with voters, celebrities seek to rule the entertainment world, fans, and paparazzi alike. Angelina Jolie has never been shy about what she wants, whether it's Billy Bob Thornton's blood or Brad Pitt's babies. When she was with Billy Bob, she proclaimed her love by wearing a vial of his blood and publicly announced that they'd just had sex in the limo, a two-for-one taboo breaker. When she fell in love with Brad Pitt on the set of *Mr. and Mrs. Smith*, she overlooked the fact that he was married to another woman at the time. When she wanted children, she got them—a lot of them— from around the world. When she wanted a divorce, she got that too. And when she completed her reformation, becoming a UN ambassador and pioneering film director, the establishment welcomed the wild child back with open arms. Passionate, provocative, and PC-defying, Angelina demands that you watch her, like it or not. In sharp contrast is Jennifer Aniston, who just happened to be the third wheel in the Angelina-Brad love triangle. Jennifer's "a very traditional feminine role model. She's nice, she's warm, she's healthy, she's natural"—so girl-next-door, in fact, that for the last decade the most persistent headlines about her revolve around whether or not she's pregnant.[5] We just don't have more to say about her.

We talk about leaders like Trump and celebrities like Angelina not because they're better or sexier than the competition but because they are who they are—good, bad, or ugly. Trump and others might well be looking for the popular vote but they're smart enough to challenge the conventional wisdom, brave enough to take *real* risks, and focused enough to put their own desires above everything else, knowing that the world will come around. They couldn't care less about what their haters say (or even what their fans say, for that matter). What makes them compelling is that they are uncompromising, polarizing, fear-inducing. They might call Trump a train wreck, but he's the only president the world couldn't take its eyes off.

Lesson of Leadership #1: Fear Is Your Friend

Awards season is a manic time for everyone in Hollywood, with all the parties, promotions, and predictions. Between events and endless interviews on my latest study, which exposed Hollywood's diversity problem in 2016—my "Hollywood is whitewashed" statement alone made headlines from *USA Today* to Yemen—I was caught up in the crazy, but not so much that I didn't notice that this year, a growing number of actors remained especially fearful of getting old, going bald, getting fired, or getting fat. I needed a break from it all and stayed in one evening to watch *The Accused*, the 1988 film that won Jodie Foster an Oscar for Best Actress. Foster's talent was undeniable, but right after the infamous rape scene, I found myself wondering if it was the gut-wrenching fear of being outed as a lesbian that drove her to take on such a risqué role— and then give the performance of her life. Like so many closeted actors in Hollywood, Foster spent years projecting a false image to the world, inevitably out of the fear of losing fans, film roles, endorsements, and ultimately her career. In Hollywood, someone is always right behind you, pushing up against you, and if you don't face your fear and stay ahead it's you who'll be doing the pushing. I believe that fear drove Foster to accomplish great things.

Yet fear is continuously labeled as a negative force, one that can only lead to violence, destruction, and distrust. From the get-go we've been told to fight it or hide it, from others and even from ourselves. We often deny fear because we're ashamed to feel it. People who use fear to rule are demonized as tyrants and dictators, and ideas that use fear to spread are quickly deemed exploitative and unethical. But what about the positive aspects of fear that have been proven, time and again, to help us reach our goals and protect us from danger?[6] If we weren't scared of the future, where would Snapchat (and its disappearing pics) be? If we weren't frightened of being alone and having no friends, then where would Facebook be? If we weren't truly afraid of missing out, would we have FaceTime? If we weren't terrified of never getting laid, where would Tinder, Grindr, or a million other "dating" apps be? Fear is an incredibly powerful force when it comes to connecting ideas and audiences. The most influential figures don't deny this reality but wholeheartedly embrace it. In doing so, they build greater self-confidence and become stronger and more authentic individuals. By using fear to your advantage, you can not only create superviral ideas but also feel superhuman.

It is better to be feared than loved.

— MACHIAVELLI

From BCE to CE to Y2K and beyond, our great leaders have used the power of fear to create culture-changing movements. Moses inspired his followers by literally putting the fear of God into them. He was less concerned about their feelings or their short-term suffering ("my damn feet hurt") than helping God keep them one step ahead of the Egyptians—and he knew his people needed to feel the fear of genocide to keep them wandering in the desert. In the buildup to World War II, Winston

Churchill rallied his troops and citizens by openly acknowledging that the coming conflict would have a huge death toll and cause British citizens unbearable pain.[7] (Compare this to our contemporary leaders' promises of how the Iraq War would "pay for itself" and we'd be "welcomed with open arms.")

As early as November 1932, Churchill painted a vivid picture at odds with post–World War I nonviolence: "All these bands of sturdy Teutonic youths, marching through the streets and roads of Germany, with the light of desire in the eyes to suffer for their Fatherland, are not looking for status. They are looking for weapons."[8] Churchill was talking to exhausted people still recovering from World War I. Roughly 2 percent of the British population died between 1914 and 1918[9]; the country was filled with spinsters, orphans, unplowed fields, and abandoned businesses. The Brits had felt enough fear to last a lifetime. They were tired of fighting, tired of death, and they simply wanted to rebuild their country as best they could. Yet Churchill didn't cover up the truth; he confided that another war was coming, and it would be just as bad as the first one or maybe worse. The future of the world hung in the balance. The Brits could have refused to follow their leader; but they had faith, believed in Churchill's wisdom, and respected his honesty. They felt the fear, embraced it, and went back to war.

An Unexpected Contest: The Dalai Lama versus Elon Musk

Shortly after awards season, I was whisked off to Milan on a private jet to meet the head of a luxury fashion house. This industry legend needed help in choosing a celebrity for his next global campaign. I was excited to get out of L.A. for a few days, especially since Milan is one of my favorite Italian cities and the fashion house was one I had admired for years.

En route, I was reading an interview in the *New York Times Magazine* wherein the interviewer questioned whether the current (fourteenth) Dalai Lama would be the last Dalai Lama.[10] I knew readers would think it was a weird question; after all, the world's most famous monk is an iconic figure, seemingly adored by all, at least in Hollywood, where Buddhism might as well be the official religion. In fact, he frequently shows up to bless rooms and kiss billionaires' babies (for which his foundation no doubt receives a generous donation). His peaceful proverbs and smiling face reassure the Bel-Air elite that they've done their part by making an appearance at the annual U.S. Tibet House Benefit Concert or by filming a nonprofit spot to persuade the rest of the world to donate to the cause. However, if the Dalai Lama really wanted to fight for his people and his culture (both currently being obliterated by the Chinese), he would get down and dirty and spread a little fear instead of self-help memes via his Instagram account. Everyone feels safe within the warm embrace of the mild-mannered Buddhist, but a true extremist for peace would find it in his ethical code to commit some extremist action.

Once you learn that the Dalai Lama is besties with Richard Gere, is on Sharon Stone's speed dial for impromptu spiritual work, and has said that a female successor is possible but that the "female must be attractive, otherwise it is not much use,"[11] it's hard to see him as the great spiritual leader we've been sold. In fact, a visual of the Dalai Lama getting real and a little enraged might well be more credible, especially considering that the state of despair in Tibet has driven "more than two dozen Buddhist monks and nuns to the deeply un-Buddhist act of public suicide."[12] What if the international icon set himself on fire in front of the White House? It would, at least, prove more newsworthy than celebrating his eightieth birthday at the Glastonbury Festival with Lionel Richie. If the Dalai Lama left us feeling less "safe" and more "fearful," he could claim to be more authentic. By acknowledging his fear, instead of pretending it doesn't exist, and addressing issues directly to the Chinese instead of resisting conflict and being "nice," the world's most famous monk could become even more famous. In fact, fear might well end up imbuing his messages with as much passion, power, and shareability as his most infamous competitor in religious ideology, ISIS.

If Tenzin Gyatso is hesitant to spread fear, infamous self-made billionaire Elon Musk is his polar opposite. Musk, Silicon Valley titan and CEO of one of the most celebrated companies in history, SpaceX, is famous for thriving on fear. His personal terror—that his companies will fail[13]—is quite literally propelling his rocket company into space. Musk feels his fear every day and makes sure his employees feel it too. Most interestingly, he defies the business school cliché of the "good" leader, yet he remains loved by the very same employees he terrifies.

Perhaps that's because, in addition to being a great fear-inducer, Musk is also frighteningly brilliant. He's in the same category as Steve Jobs, but perhaps even more fascinating and revolutionary. He's reshaped the way we shop (PayPal), get around (Tesla is currently the only commercially viable alternative technology car company, and his proposed Hyperloop may one day make the trip from Los Angeles to San Francisco a thirty-minute train ride), and dream (reopening the possibility of sending a human to Mars). Ultimately, Musk believes he can help build a multiplanet civilization, even if he doesn't live long enough to see it himself.[14]

Humility is no substitute for a good personality.

—FRAN LEBOWITZ

From day 1 at SpaceX, when there were fewer than one hundred employees and the company hadn't even launched a successful payload, Musk's goal was the same: get a human to Mars. "Jim Cantrell, SpaceX's first engineer, says of Musk, 'The guy is pure ambition. He's three or four steps ahead. . . . Most of us can't conceive of these things working; he can't conceive of it failing. Period.' This is the hallmark of an opinionated leader."[15] Musk's leadership style has defied the conventional wisdom of baby steps to prevent cultural disruption and small, incremental goals. His agenda is personal, which explains why he has little interest in taking his company public and reporting to others. Musk's brand of leadership is not about earnings but ideas, not about consensus-building but the courage of his convictions. Despite the fear and enormous focus on Musk, the first thing newcomers to SpaceX ask their colleagues is, according to a fellow Oxford University alum and senior SpaceX employee, "Have you met Elon?" The experience of working at SpaceX is all about Elon; even the SpaceX brand comes a distant second to the man himself.

Musk is terrifying both as an individual and as an idea, and his businesses are littered with the burnt-out remains of engineers encouraged to work hundred-hour weeks on projects that were promptly cancelled.[16] His first wife was cut loose after a brutal divorce, and legend has it that one employee was blasted for taking a day off to witness the birth of his child (Musk vehemently denies this). Yet he is also utterly committed to his vision. In 2008, in the wake of the stock market crash and auto industry bailout, he invested his entire personal fortune into the suddenly struggling Tesla and SpaceX.[17] SpaceX has, since its inception, successfully launched fifteen rockets, signed a multibillion-dollar contract with NASA, and leased the iconic 39A launch pad at Cape Canaveral, home of the original Apollo missions.[18] However, Musk still remains alone in his vision of a successful manned mission to mars. NASA is not aggressively working toward a Mars mission, and conventional wisdom in the aeronautical industry tells us the closest we will ever get to the red planet are virtual reality robotic explorations controlled by astronauts in orbit around Mars.[19] Mars's and Earth's varying orbits mean that a mission is potentially possible only when the two planets are within relatively close reach of each other. The next alignment will be four years from now and then again in the mid-2030s, when Elon Musk will be in his mid-sixties. If SpaceX misses that window then Musk most likely will not live long enough to see another. Yet he's still a believer. His fear of not realizing his Mars vision has inspired him to attempt the seemingly impossible.

In our struggle for freedom, truth is the only weapon we possess.

—THE FOURTEENTH DALAI LAMA

If the Dalai Lama appears focused on the needs of others, Musk, in contrast, is utterly focused on his own needs. And while we often feel the need to demonize these types of leaders as arrogant or assholes, divas or delusional—and secretly hope for their downfall—those who focus on themselves and use fear in their struggle to get ahead are not only redefining our culture but also inspiring others to shape the future. According to the old-school definition of "good," they are indeed "bad." But today being bad requires being brave, and it is this truth that will enhance your credibility, humanity, and authenticity as a leader. If the Dalai Lama took a page out of Elon Musk's book and realized that the need to befriend Beyoncé was indeed his truth, he wouldn't need the PR spin of peace.

He'd let us in on some real post-party Instagram action, and, like Elon, truly change the world.

The Science of Fear

When we fear things I think we wish for them . . . every fear embodies a wish.

—DAVID MAMET

A vacation exposed me to some much-needed Miami heat, and I soon found myself on a superyacht with a world-famous model and renowned businessman. It wasn't long before I started grilling him on his drive and creative vision. He told me that fear had been a powerfully creative and protective force in his life—he was always willing to listen to his fears. We spoke of how, when he was a young teenager from a broken home, fear kept him away from the edge of a cliff. It was fear that drove him to put in that one last all-nighter to pass his exams as a student. It was the fear of losing his partner that told him to say no to his last drink. And it was his fear of the sea and sailing that inspired him to get his eighty-five-foot gin bin. Happily, fear is not a rational thing. If fear worked logically, it would make us sick and desperate to get as far away from the source of distress as possible. But this man had reached a point where his fear felt *good*. In fact, our brains respond to dangerous and exciting situations by pumping us full of adrenaline and releasing a mix of feel-good chemicals into our bloodstream.[20]

Our brains cannot differentiate between genuinely frightening experiences and those that have been designed to scare us for fun. When we seek out the feeling of fear through scary movies, roller coasters, and haunted houses, we're looking for a hit of adrenaline or dopamine while knowing we aren't in any real danger. However, in the case of extreme sports, the real chance of a chilling outcome is part of the thrill of playing and watching.[21]

Scientists show that people who call themselves thrill-seekers get a bigger hit of dopamine from such activities than their less adventurous peers, which explains why many climbers, skydivers, and stunt riders are so dedicated to the cause: fear might literally be addictive.[22] Free solo climbers (crazy climbing without any ropes or safety gear) like Alex Honnold have spoken about their intimate relationships with fear, and famed bicycle stunt rider Matt Hoffman says, "Fear gives you that extra energy that gets 110 percent out of you."[23] Fear is intertwined with ecstasy, and for some it's the difference between living and simply existing.

Likewise, any artist, writer, or musician knows that the creative process can be terrifying. Fear forces you to face the possibility that you have nothing worth saying, painting, or singing—and this sensation is at its most powerful during the positive procrastination stage, or "incubation" as it's been termed by psychologist Graham Wallas. Our fear of failure, and the positive procrastination period it generates, are essential to the creative process. They allow our ideas to evolve in our minds and prevent us from making rushed decisions or killing our ideas too quickly.[24] True creativity and fear go hand in hand. They require you to push yourself, to step away from your familiar thought patterns into unknown territory, often a scary feat in itself.

A study recently published in the *British Journal of Criminology* shows that the fear of crime has a positive effect. People who are especially afraid of crime are the most likely to take precautions and change the way they interact with their

environment.[25] Their fear—a supposedly negative emotion—
has the ultimate effect of making them safer. Similarly, those
who fear an outcome during a critical waiting process, such as
exam results, are better able to cope with the resulting good or
bad news. In fact, those who meditate on their fear during the
waiting process are also more motivated to bounce back into action in the event of bad news than those who push their fears
aside in an effort to remain positive (and end up in a state of
disbelief).[26]

**Forget everything and run or face everything
and rise.**

—Zig Ziglar

Fear will set you free, not love. The first step toward creating
leading ideas is to be fearless about embracing that truth. If
your idea uses fear and in turn communicates honestly and
authentically, it will directly engage audiences in a powerful
and resonant way—regardless of whether others label it dangerous or destructive, or brand you a bastard or a bitch. Fear
is the harsh reality of our culture. So embrace your fear, love
it, share it, and allow it to break down the barriers between what we say and what we actually do.

Lesson of Leadership #2: No Compromises

**Indeed the safest road to Hell is the gradual
one.**

—C. S. Lewis

When the UK's top celebrity gossip magazine, *Heat*, asked me if I was surprised that Candice Brown was crowned the winner of *The Great British Bake Off*, I had to admit that I wasn't. While the other contestants were busy adapting their styles to please the judges, I noticed how Candice stood firm in her own mission, to go above and beyond, and bake for herself. When she was told to make a three-tier cake, she made four. When her closest competitor decided to cut loose and go with the flow, Candice's eye remained on the prize. As I told *Heat*, it was this attitude that separated the Star Baker from her highly skilled competitors, crowned her the winner, and gives her the potential to be Britain's next Nigella Lawson.

"If you want to get along, you have to go along" is a sweet sentiment from JFK, but one that has less of a place than ever in today's world of fierce competition, fighters for equality, and audiences that prize authenticity above anything else. Although the world has grown in complexity since the era of JFK and Camelot (#LoveIsLove now after all), we still abide by some seriously simple ideas about the ultimate key to happiness. Compromise results in a "win-win" situation where everyone gets a little bit of what they want. If people don't compromise, we label them as unreasonable or difficult. But what about the mystery man who said, "A compromise is an agreement whereby both parties get what neither of them wanted"?

Those who fall for compromise end up in the best case not quite getting what they wanted or in the worst case feeling entirely, well, "compromised." Contrary to what JFK would have us believe, today compromise *is* cowardice, negotiation is negation, and humility is a has-been, especially if you need to succeed against all odds.

Many of the street-smart leaders in Tinseltown have been spared from the indoctrination of years of B-school rote learning, standardized testing, and compromise coaching. Instead, they've learned how to live, lead, and learn in Hollywood. I quickly learned that people who get ahead here don't compromise, and they certainly don't possess the checklist of Harvard leadership characteristics that make someone a "good" or "bad" person: humility, empathy, generosity, kindness—say what? Instead, their skins are thickened by constantly being judged by others: "difficult," "intimidating," "demanding." Despite the criticism, they stick to their guns. Many come out on top, and if they get exposed or torn down, so be it. Kathryn Bigelow is among the "most daring and artistically respected filmmakers," but she also has "a reputation for antagonizing cast and crew and alienating important allies." In other words, she's a bitch. She also has an Oscar for best director on *The Hurt Locker* (and is the only winner among the four female directors who have ever been nominated). Although one of her earlier films, *K-19,* went belly-up at the box office, the Paramount exec who acquired it had nothing but praise for her. "She executed it brilliantly. . . . If it didn't make a lot of money, blame it on us. Kathryn is a giant talent and always has been. She's always been uncompromising and always had a vision."[27] Hollywood makes one thing clear—chasing your dreams doesn't require compromise; it requires sacrifice, plain and simple.

Art Is No Compromise

> Learn the rules like a pro so you can break them like an artist.
>
> —PABLO PICASSO

If you want to learn about the perils and payoffs of being uncompromising, there is no better place to look than the world

of art. Be they painters, writers, or poets, many of our leading artistic icons hold fast to their integrity, only to be ridiculed during their lifetimes and celebrated as visionaries only
after their deaths. My personal favorites among these are the
metaphysical poets, especially John Donne.

John Donne, Andrew Marvel, and Henry Vaughan were
the original bad boys of rhyme. They blew apart the idea of
how a poem could be structured, what it should celebrate,
and how it should make the reader feel. These brilliant men
were not only witty and disarming but also deeply conflicted
in the way they saw the world. Like many of us, they were
overthinkers, but unlike their peers, the metaphysical poets
were meta because of their utterly uncompromising ideas.

Donne's poetry was long dismissed as crass and talentless.[28]
Like the dating apps of today, Donne was more of a cut-to-
the-chase kind of guy, and proud of it. In one poem he uses
the occasion of a flea hopping between himself and a young
woman he is eyeing up to justify getting laid. After all, inside
the flea, their blood is already mixed together. Donne's on-
point yet nonjudgmental description of how desire disappears
once it is consummated—"Being had, enjoying it decays"[29]—
could have been drawn straight from the Tinder-generation
playbook. He combined spiritual love with the physical need
to shag by laughing at the women he seduced, yet he wrote
passionately about his love for his somewhat nerdy wife,
Anne More. In the end, his uncompromising nature left him
conflicted between his spiritual and physical pursuits, and
that tension became the source of his bravery, creativity, and
much buzz.

Donne's lessons in tenacity, authenticity, and intention are
as valid today as they were four hundred years ago. Although
Donne was admired among his contemporaries, he had plenty
of haters. The result of Donne putting his own need to express

himself above the rules was that his poetry was more open to interpretation than that of his contemporaries. Audiences related to Donne because he wasn't prescriptive but freeing.

Donne's realness was often deemed too provocative for refined ears—in almost exactly the same way that Kim Kardashian is seen as too crass for sophisticated people to take seriously. When *Cosmopolitan* called the Kardashians "America's first family," it sparked an immediate backlash. Some Americans were plainly disgusted, while others thought it disrespectful to the real first family of America, the Obamas. I was asked for my opinion by the media. As I told CBS, not only are the Kardashians America's *first* family but they are our second and third family too. They are a bona fide cultural phenomenon. Perhaps, like John Donne, future critics will learn to respect Kim's uncompromising commentary on contemporary culture—though I doubt that Kim and her Kohorts will have the patience to wait.

Passion Is Fashion

If you can't walk in them, then don't wear them.

—CHRISTIAN LOUBOUTIN

In order to succeed in Hollywood, you need to be uncompromising in your loyalty, your discipline, your dreams, and your dress sense. In fact, I landed my first job offer in showbiz because the CEO took a liking to my Dior Homme suit and my overall "look." I found this somewhat strange. Why would someone be so drawn toward the way I looked and dressed? Did it really matter? I soon realized that in a town where perception is everything, your image is related to your ability to influence. Still, regardless of other people's positive or negative image of me, what mattered was my own image of myself. My suit was as much about my style as it was about my success: it was indicative of the risks I took in the boardroom, on camera, and in the classroom. Tinseltown taught me that an uncompromising sense of style would not only get you noticed but also allow you to negotiate your way through anything.

Uncompromising ideas are often the most powerful innovations and game changers. These ideas don't just tap into the culture but remake it in their own image. And it doesn't get more uncompromising than the shoes of French designer Christian Louboutin, who is both credited with and blamed for inventing the killer stiletto. "Loubies" are best known for their extreme height and price. Heels can ascend to a dizzying six inches in height, and the crystal-covered Sexy Strass will set you back a mere $3,095. Easily identified by their signature scarlet sole—Pantone 18, Chinese Red to be exact—history's hottest high heels are designed not for walking but wooing. In fact, Loubies promise to not only increase the contour of your leg but also arch your foot—in the same manner as you would in the throes of ecstasy—getting many to believe that the price tag came with an orgasm. Big O or not, there is no other stiletto that makes so much noise and generates such deep emotions. *Vogue* editor at large Hamish Bowles noted, "There's the promise of something wicked in Christian's shoes. They're a little dangerous, and there's a sense of teetering on the precipice between avoiding dreary conventional good taste and tumbling into something far more outrageous."[30]

Louboutin's most iconic high heel is the Pigalle 120. Strictly for the intermediate to advanced wearer, the shoe's shiny black S&M aesthetic is undeniable. The number 120 refers to each millimeter of spiked heel that has come to symbolize both power and submission. The remaining design of the Pigalle is equally provocative. The heel's extreme height is matched by the lowness of the front vamp, which reveals an undeniably sexual expanse of toe cleavage. The sides of the shoe similarly hang low to reveal an aggressive curvature that demands the foot be bent at the toes to a ninety-degree angle. Needless to say, moving in these nearly five-inch-high stilettos of fine Italian leather is practically impossible.

The Pigalle's flash of red is de rigueur for rising starlets, established stars, and trophy wives who can bear to walk the walk in 90210 (as are her even more extreme sisters, the Allenissima and the Hot Chick). J. Lo dedicated an entire song to the brand and the enhancing impact of the red bottoms on her booty. However, not all women have succumbed to the highly sexual allure of the killer heel. I remember how at the seventy-first Golden Globe awards, British actress Emma Thompson walked on stage barefoot with her Louboutins in one hand (and a martini in the other), comparing the red soles to her blood, only to throw them over her shoulder before announcing the award for best screenplay. Regardless, it's the burning desire to wear them, woo in them, and power play in them that separates the lovers from the haters.

High heels have always been highly sexualized, but Louboutin was the first high-end shoe designer to embrace fetishism in such an open way. His made-to-measure Ballerina Ultima took his passion for fetish to its logical conclusion. The Ultima, designed with David Lynch in 2007, is the tallest heel ever created by the shoe designer and pushes the wearer's feet into the extreme shape of a ballerina's foot en pointe. "If there is an element of fetishism in a wardrobe, it is the female shoe, even without stilettos," said Louboutin. "It is an object of worship that lead [*sic*] to rituals."[31]

His bondage aesthetic of spikes, studs, and lace promises sexual power and possibility but demands undying devotion—

much like the dungeon master and his perfect slave. A-list celebrities from Lady Gaga to Victoria Beckham have lusted for Louboutin, but like a good master he will not give his love away for free. Jaqueline Steele, his most devoted customer, has a dedicated closet of over six thousand pairs of Loubies, and women of all economic and social backgrounds are ready to drool at the first signs of the sadistic yet seductive shoe.

Monsieur Louboutin, with his penchant for ignoring safe words, is astute in going to extremes that other designers are hesitant to consider, and his uncompromising strategy has paid off. He's brave enough to recognize that he can't "be all things to all people" and focuses on a specific group of women who love to both give it and take it. He's had to fight off imitators from YSL (which was eventually allowed to continue producing its red-all-over stilettos[32]) and Charles Jourdan from DSW (which wasn't). He probably doesn't care if you love or hate his shoes, but at the same time he is aware of the full range of attitudes toward his products and remains true to his own inflexible point of view. "I don't think of comfort when I'm designing a shoe," declares Louboutin, in a world where people supposedly want it all. In 2012 Louboutin sold over seven hundred thousand pairs of shoes, and among the holy trinity of luxury footwear, including Manolo Blahnik and Jimmy Choo, Louboutin and his hard-nosed strategy comes out on top.

The Lady is not for turning.

—MARGARET THATCHER

So while you're constantly reminded that reasonable people make compromises and the c-word turns up time and again on the top-ten list of leadership characteristics, the fact of the matter remains that in a world of changing rules, the act of compromise has turned into a dangerous game. Audiences want to know what you think, how you feel, and what you stand for. And *that* is the definition of emotional intelligence that resonates with audiences today. Nothing is more compelling than a person with complete faith in their convictions. That is the sine qua non of leading ideas today. I've learned it's less about self-regulation and more about self-confidence. It's not about being comfortable with others but first showing that you are comfortable with yourself. It's not about a focus on others; it's about a focus on yourself and your bullshit in all its glory. After all, you can't fake chemistry, and you can't turn on other people if you're not turned on yourself.

Lesson of Leadership #3: The Power of Being Polarizing

If you're not polarizing, you failed, in my opinion.

—MIRANDA LAMBERT

"That nigger just wants white pussy," a studio exec told me one night over drinks at the Chateau Marmont. It wasn't the first time I had heard the word being used around town by powerful non-black men. Even celebrities like John Mayer, Paris Hilton, and Hulk Hogan were users of the term.[33] But I still choked on my old-fashioned, and it wasn't a good look at the Chateau, hideaway for the perfectly poised. In England, we didn't even use slang, let alone the "N-Bomb." Saying "TV" instead of "television" was enough to get detention at my traditional all-boys school. But this wasn't Downton Abbey, it was Hollywood. Rather than demonize others for their bigotry, I started thinking about the power of an extreme perspective to express yourself and break through—not in the "right" way, as determined by others' standards, but in your way, by *your* standards.

The world is a place of extremes, and Hollywood is its proving ground: the extreme makeover, the extreme diet, the extreme cosmetic surgery. Forget religious zealots or presidential candidates; if you want evidence of just how far truly passionate people will go to achieve their aims, just look at the beauty regime of the average B-lister. Whether it's the self-consuming vampire facelift (take a vial of the individual's blood, separate it to isolate the platelet-rich fibrin matrix, then inject it back into the face—Kim K's bloody procedure was filmed for *Kim and Kourtney Take Miami*), bee venom face mask, or earthworm "compost" supplements, the young and the restless will go to extreme lengths to prop up their falling features and fading careers.

Hollywood divas (of all genders) do this because succeeding in an industry as competitive as Tinseltown is no joke. No one is going to reward ambivalence or half-heartedness. Silver screen glory requires you to go all the way in everything you do. This philosophy might seem obvious for Oscar-caliber work—Heath Ledger's Joker or Leonardo DiCaprio's tortured woodsman in *The Revenant*[34]—but it's equally true for actors sweating away on instantly forgettable films—Michael J. Fox almost hung himself during a botched execution scene in *Back to the Future III*.[35] Surely a movie is not worth dying for. But Hollywood teaches us the power of being polarizing.

There is more pressure than ever to conform, so you have to be extreme to get ahead. You must make a stand about who you are and what you have to say. People may hate you or love you, but they certainly won't ignore you. Extremists are the innovators, the ones with the balls to put their ideas out there and the strength to withstand the tide of public opinion.

Aim to Offend

I will not stay silent so that you can stay
comfortable.

—MARTIN LUTHER KING JR.

Like most Brits, I grew up in sheer terror of causing offense.
Stepping out of line was unimaginable. I was raised to be
polite, agree with my elders, and never kiss and tell. At
Harvard Business School the same sentiment prevailed.
Leaders needed to be consistent and reliable and wear blue
shirts and khaki pants. Women never dared to wear skirts
that rose above the knee. I learned to speak diplomatically,
both internally and externally, and to repress my true
thoughts and feelings. My responsibility was not to myself
but to my future company's shareholders. Rather than being
transparent and open, I was taught to be a consensus builder
and team player.

However, in today's increasingly skeptical environment
where it's harder than ever to truly resonate with your audience, no one believes a word of corporate communications, and
audiences throw up at the first sign of a contrived statement.
As a result, the sheer power of speaking your mind and being
unafraid to offend has never been greater.

At the same time, the power of leaders has grown exponentially. And in a world of nonstop media, traditional, digital and otherwise, leaders are far less distant than in past
generations. We are now determined to suss out their inner
thoughts, opinions, and limitations in order to work out their
modus operandi. We no longer separate the person from the

job. After the scandal of VW (Dieselgate, the rigging of U.S. exhaust emissions tests), among others, exposed how leaders were saying all the right things but doing something very different, audiences are officially over it. Indeed, the value of an honest and open conversation is greater than any PR-proofed public announcement.

Many organizations are using the freedom to offend as a strategic competitive advantage. Urban Outfitters continues to corner the market in clothing and accessories that generate outrageous opinions and significant sales. From its blood-stained Kent State sweatshirt to its Navaho panties, the "Tranny" greeting card and the "Eat Less" tee, the retailer leaves no stone unturned in its search for iconography or ideas that get people pissed, get in the news, and drive traffic to its stores and website. Offense is the new sexy, and if you want people to care then you've got to feel free to offend.

Aiming to offend can prove to be even more worthwhile for women and other minority groups who are less likely to speak their mind. Outgunned in the business world, blacks, Latinos, and women report feeling isolated in what remains a stereotypically all-white, all-boys boardroom. However, they also feel less comfortable with the idea of antagonizing their coworkers, and as a result their true opinions often go unheard. More concerned about being judged or upsetting other people, women are also less likely to interrupt a conversation and speak their mind,[36] so their silence is conveniently taken as an agreement. Who can forget Patricia Arquette's speech at the 2015 Oscars on gender equality and the wage gap between women and men? It was a perfect example of aiming to offend, and it struck a nerve worldwide.

And we had better get used to pushing each other's buttons because audiences can't get enough of it. Right now, "Run the Gauntlet" is blowing up subReddits, gaming forums, and 4chan. Self-described as "the most vile, puke-inducing, hard-to-watch videos on the Internet," "Run the Gauntlet" is a progressive daisy chain of disturbing videos that push the envelope of offensive to the outer limits. If you make it all the way through the first video (a young woman's arm being snapped in a wrestling contest), you can watch the second video, and so on. Later videos show death, dismemberment, acts of torture, and horrifying accidents. Interestingly, most of the website's traffic comes from America, although Americans are the least willing to admit to watching the videos, whereas viewers in Thailand and Hong Kong have no problem hitting the "Run the Gauntlet" Like button on Facebook.[37]

What's more, despite strong evidence to the contrary, audiences today hold on to unbelievable opinions. Researchers at the University of Michigan find that when "misinformed people . . . were exposed to corrected facts in news stories, they rarely changed their minds. In fact, they often became even more strongly set in their beliefs."[38] For instance, even though Barack Obama presented his long-form birth certificate in 2011, many Americans still refuse to believe he is a U.S. citizen. Despite mountains of scientific data and visible, real-time realities like the melting Arctic, a significant few still deny the reality of global warming. Polarizing opinion battles run wild on social media. Audiences are demanding stronger viewpoints that they can either love or hate, and as a result are dictating a new playbook for those interested in creating breakthrough ideas. Whether it's "Run the Gauntlet" or the Rich Kids of Instagram showing off their decadent parties and designer shopping hauls with daddy's money, today you've got to be willing to take a stand, make a statement, and offend because just as you are offending millions of people, you will likewise be enthralling many millions more.

Nice Guys Should *Finish Last*

> Once you accept another person's authority,
> you become a different person, you are con-
> cerned with how well you follow out your
> orders, rather than whether it is right or wrong.
>
> — Dr. Thomas Blass

The morning after drinks at the Chateau Marmont, I woke up with my head spinning and the sound of my cell phone exploding; it was a series of frantic texts from the chief marketing officer of a consumer packaged goods company. He had bet big on a celebrity endorsement thanks to guidance from his advertising agency, and when the campaign launched in the summer months, when sales were expected to increase, they actually took a nosedive. Josh was stumped. The celebrity he had chosen was super popular, squeaky clean, and seemingly liked by everyone, and she had never been caught shoplifting or snorting coke (at least on camera). And therein lay the problem.

Playing it safe can be tempting in life, but in business it isn't going to get you anywhere. Polarization is an essential and powerful tool, one that gives you the strength to be yourself in a cultural environment that demands conformity. The classic Milgram experiment proved that seemingly rational "good" guys are only too willing to torture each other when instructed to do so by an authority figure. An astonishing 65 percent of study participants were willing to give supposedly dangerous and painful electric shocks to people simply because they were told to do so. A 2014 repeat performance of the experiment found that agreeable people tend to avoid breaking the rules and upsetting others, and more easily comply with social expectations.[39] Even when those demands are unthinkable.

Of course there's nothing new about using the power of perceived authority to get nice people to do not-so-nice things. For the most part, civilian members of the Nazi party were friendly, pleasant, and eager to just get along. Forget Himmler or Goebbels. As philosopher Hannah Arendt claimed in *Eichmann in Jerusalem*, the power of the party came from its millions of everyday members and their fundamental desire to fit in, to not rock the boat. The "crime had become for the criminals accepted, routinised, and implemented without moral revulsion and political indignation and resistance."[40] In other words, the danger of the Nazis came from their willingness to delegate thinking, decision making, and even morality to their superiors.

That kind of mindless compliance continues today, with seriously harmful consequences. In 2004, thirty-eight-year-old prison guard David Stewart was arrested in Panama City, Florida. Over the previous ten years (and as documented in the 2012 indie film *Compliance*), scammers had repeatedly used prepaid calling cards to dial fast-food restaurants in small towns or rural neighborhoods (because they were "more trusting"). He then impersonated a police officer and convinced the shift managers to carry out invasive strip searches of teenage employees.[41] They targeted the highly regimented "by the book" restaurant chains because they knew that if they could get the naïve managers to go "off the book" and deal with a situation they hadn't been trained for, they would be lost. The managers were easily manipulated and persuaded to do things that—if they were thinking clearly, or thinking at all—they would never comply with.[42] Mr Stewart? He was acquitted of impersonating a policeman during a phone call to a McDonald's and talking the managers into sexually abusing an eighteen-year-old female employee after a weeklong trial. So the culprit is still out there, and it seems there are many others operating the same scam playing on people's compliance.

If we've learned anything from cold-calling creeps or the millions of Nazi minions who willingly collaborated with the Third Reich's master plan, it's the importance of being offensive, having strong opinions, and being willing to shout them from the rooftops. When we are willing to offend, we are willing to stand up for our beliefs, to risk being unpopular or even shunned, rather than go along with something we know is wrong. It turns out that offensive, disagreeable, and stubborn behaviors are profoundly "pro-social" and that a healthy, successful society *requires* some people to be unpopular.[43] This is important not only for individuals but also for ideas, products, and services. Nothing can please everyone. You can't compel your audience to like you by abusing the power of perceived authority—that is, telling them what to like and why. Instead, you have to feel free to show them your true colors and let them make up their own minds.

Love Your Haters

> Haters are my favorite. I've built an empire
> with the bricks they've thrown at me. Keep on
> hating.
>
> —CM PUNK

When the *Independent* asked me to give my verdict on the Queen of Pop, Madonna, I received more than my usual amount of fan mail on social media: "Dude, this article is pure garbage and a clear waste of time"; "Whoever wrote this shit should have their eyes cut out"; "Who gives a fuck what this WANKER thinks." You get the point. But the reality is that those haters reacted so negatively toward me because they recognized the power in what I was saying and how much it was resonating around the world.

Whether you are team Madonna or Gaga, Midwesterners or West Coasters, culturally conservative or liberally progressive, Sunni or Shiite, you will occasionally feel that your way of life is in danger of extinction—of being overrun by "others." Depending on your perspective, these "others" can be people of other races, people of other belief systems, or simply people whose personal habits and peccadillos you don't like. You have two options. Either empathize and find common ground with these others or—more often—find reasons to distrust and hate each other. But suppose that hate, rather than a bad thing, is actually a liberating and powerful tool—one that can give you insight into yourself and help you develop a more honest and open relationship with your customers, fans, friends, and family. Maybe you've always been trained to avoid hate by being told to rise above it, but what happens if you embrace the hate and learn to love it?

Haters can be some of your most powerful motivators, and there are key benefits of being on the receiving end of serious hate. Any product, idea, or individual needs honest, unfiltered, and immediate feedback, yet this is often very difficult to get from consumers. But now, among the trolls, the tweeters, and the 4chaners, are people who hate you enough to blog, tweet, or hashtag their dislike. These hits, even when they're unflattering, can be insightful. When McDonald's asked fans what they loved about #RonaldMcDonald, they were bombarded with tweets about underpaid labor, animal cruelty, and poor nutrition. Not exactly the response the corporation was looking for—and they probably should have seen it coming—but they gained valuable insights into where they were going wrong with millions of potential fans. Listen to your haters and—more importantly—learn from them.

If you're not being hated, then you're not really in the game. Hate is a form of engagement, and in an environment where most people are too busy to engage at all, hate means you are at least connecting on a deep enough level to inspire a response. MRIs show that hate activates the same area of the brain (the frontal cortex) as romantic love.[44] When we are hated, it is because we are doing something so extreme, shocking, or exciting that it incites an emotional response from our audience.

Adidas's #therewillbehaters campaign used soccer player Luis Suarez—known for his eight game ban after being accused of racially abusing Patrice Evra during a match (which he denies and blames on the mistranslation of the word from Portuguese), not to mention his occasional violent outbursts on the pitch—to start a bigger conversation about hate with its customers. "It was a 'bold' move for Adidas . . . but forced the company to talk to customers directly and authentically about hatred, rather than outsource to agencies."[45] While this might seem less relevant to the job of selling shoes, the conversation created a stronger feeling of intimacy and connection between the brand and customers.

Haters can end up being—conversely—your most powerful advocates. After all, nothing inspires a passionate Twitter rant in your defense from the people who love what you are doing like an enraged detractor. Use the hate to increase the love by getting your die-hard fans to support you stronger, and for longer. It's harder to win over new customers than it is to keep existing customers and turn them into more-committed advocates. Consider the possibility that haters are not your problem and avoiding them is.

The Excitement of Polarizing Your Life

A fanatic is one who can't change his mind
and won't change the subject.

— WINSTON CHURCHILL

After a few months of studying Madonna, I felt the need to step up my game at the gym. I needed a serious release, so I decided to finally cave in and give SoulCycle a try. I've been addicted ever since, but many of my friends prefer Flywheel. I never thought my own obsession with indoor cycling would interfere with my friendships, or that preferring SoulCycle to Flywheel would be tantamount to choosing sides in the Civil War. But this is Hollywood, where working out is a religion and choosing a gym is far more serious than choosing a mate or a political candidate.

Big ideas that build lasting connections have to be deeply polarizing, and SoulCycle is no exception. For every super-model who swears by the spiritual spin class, there are thousands of gym-goers who are turned off by its cultlike atmosphere and clublike waitlist, and that's before they even get to the cost of a class. SoulCycle understands the power of being polarizing: you can't be loved by everyone, so it's better to be the object of the obsession of a special few. People are desperate to be admitted to the class, where the studios are dark, hot, and sweaty, and the music is deafening. As the class progresses, "everyone is in a stunned, near-hallucinatory state, and suddenly [the instructor's] banter sounds utterly profound." Finding your soul "involves getting everyone hopped up on a cocktail of cardio fitness, motivational sayings, and the frisson of excitement that comes from overpaying for something worthwhile."[46]

Like any good religion, SoulCycle isn't interested in cultivating fans, only die-hard followers. These devotees not only derive a sense of identity, community, and belonging from the experience but also a big boost of self-esteem. " 'If you weren't sexy, confident, and strong, you wouldn't be here,' says cult trainer Stacey Griffith as the crowd pumps away on stationary bikes. . . . 'You're all sexy,' she shouts. 'This is a sexy-ass sport right here!' "[47] You don't just get a better ass, but an entire value system. And, like religion, the spirituality of spin is deeply divisive. Soulies defend themselves when attacked and remain loyal even if prices are jacked up further. Some ride multiple times a day and, as in the case of Lady Gaga, take custom-made bikes on tour and celebrate their birthday at the studio. Others buy the Supersoul package, which includes fifty classes, for $3,500. Most importantly, Soulies are decked out in SoulCycle gear, including their neon-emblazoned logos like "posse," "cult," and "obsessed off duty," and they are always ready to ride, rinse, and repeat.

Big, polarizing ideas also build some major immunity. While SoulCycle's brand of workout might well nourish the soul, it's been heavily criticized for potentially doing the opposite to the body. The mechanics of the workout—the minimal weights used to tone the upper body and the "out of the seat" push-ups and dance moves—allegedly decrease the effectiveness of the cycling itself. Some movements are supposedly bad for your back. Couple this with neither of its founders having a background in health (one being an ex-Hollywood talent manager and the other a high-end real estate agent), and you could make a good case for style but not substance, all of which is denied by the owners. Yet none of this matters to the devotees, who believe they gain much more than a workout, and SoulCycle continues to conquer the world.

> It's good to break the mold and then recreate one.
>
> —KIM KARDASHIAN

In a culture where leadership and celebrity have commingled, there is no doubt that Kim Kardashian is a new world leader. Defined by her refusal to be defined—"I've just had enough of people misrepresenting me. Get to know me and see who I am"—Kim has successfully aligned legions of followers to both love her and hate her. Business leaders have been straight-jacketed for far too long, spoon-fed "carefully" crafted phrases to repeat like robots in difficult times—these phrases once worked but now fall on deaf ears—and are programmed how to think, act, and even feel.

Kim resonates with audiences because she has infused pur-pose and meaning into the life of others. She's all about going out and getting what you want: "If I don't feel confident about my body, I'm not going to sit at home and feel sorry for my-self and not do something about it. It's all about taking action and not being lazy. So you do the work, whether it's fitness or whatever. It's about getting up, motivating yourself and just doing it." Compared to other celebrities, Kim is seen as some-one who is not only shaping the future but also building the next generation of fans. On the one hand, she has built her brand within the traditional framework of celebrity with a reality TV show. On the other hand, she has been able to reflect on the current framework of fame and find ways to fundamentally improve and amplify her fame across social media, games, and other brand extensions. You need two hands and a lot of commitment; this capability is the essence of successful leadership.

My research into the nature of Kim Kardashian's celebrity reveals that those who say Kim Kardashian's mother, Kris Jenner, is the puppet master also say Kim Kardashian knows exactly what she wants and rank her similarly to the profile of a person in control of her life. Four in five people agree that she is a shrewd businesswoman. These same people also agree that a mega celebrity becomes a business and most likely has a team behind them. Those who claim that Kim Kardashian is a bad role model for kids in truth believe that kids are less impressionable today and are too savvy to blindly follow any one celebrity. They also believe that kids only follow celebrities who truly resonate with them. They also claim to have three times as much respect for those celebrities who have extended their brand over three or more platforms.

There is no doubt that Kim instills fear in many people. Some fear her as a vision of a future they can't bear to see. But it's this exact fear that drives people to pay attention and helps her resonate with younger audiences. She refuses to compromise, regardless of the blowback, and she's not afraid to offend. Yet the real power of Kim's influence as a leader comes from not being appointed by the establishment but by the people. Love Kim or hate her, you can't escape her. Your ideas need to be just as uncompromising, polarizing, and fear-inducing as Kim if you want them to break through the clutter of convention and find their own fans.

CHAPTER 5

Flaws

There is a crack in everything,

that's how the light gets in.

—LEONARD COHEN

Hollywood is the stuff that dreams are made of . . . but over the years, I've learned there's more than a dash of deception too. At a party for the mommy-porn movie of the year, *Fifty Shades of Grey*, I met a fascinating man named Matt. At first he was tight-lipped about his work, but after a few martinis I discovered he was a magician, only of the Hollywood variety: he worked for a studio in Photoshopping moving images. So, just as magazines touch up still images to give actors and models smaller noses, thinner waistlines, and bigger hair, some movies have their own touch-up teams. This practice remains one of Hollywood's best-kept secrets. And while Matt's client list is L.A. confidential, I was lucky enough to get an invite to the studio that night, where I witnessed a Hollywood heart-throb's biceps grow, define, tan, and defy time. It wasn't quite the Hulk-like transformation I was expecting—in fact, it was tedious and technical—but it was a master class in the deception of perfection. Frame by frame, I saw the actor transform into the action hero we all recognise. Such a shame that Jamie Dornan's super-defined six-pack, whether Photoshopped or real, didn't save the film from getting critically panned.

However, whether Hollywood realizes it or not, the tide is changing. Perfection is passé. Despite the promises of advertising, no one today believes that either stars or the products they sell are perfect. The leaked pics of L'Oréal's undoctored Beyoncé ad and her not-so-flawless skin put that fantasy to rest. Audiences have finally lost their innocence. Just as we know that neither Olay Regenerist nor Crème De La Mer will make us look ten or even two years younger.

Herein lies the paradox we face in the twenty-first century. Audiences now realize the images that surround them are no longer "real." Yet we're smack in the middle of a cultural shift away from the artificial and toward the authentic (remember Lizzy Grant–cum–Lana Del Rey, who was labeled a "fake orgasm" and never forgiven for her manufactured eccentricity?). Ideas, products, and services that try to be perfect are not cool. This shift has created enormous opportunities for people who know how to bring their flaws to life in an exciting way.

I'm like everybody else: weak, full of mistakes, but basically good.

—JUNOT DÍAZ

When Kim Kardashian shared an Instagram post of herself in the middle of a contouring session, the *New York Times* asked me for my perspective. Kim's face was covered in unblended stripes and blocks of highlighter, concealer, and various shades of contouring crèmes. It wasn't an image you'd expect an A-lister to share, and that's what made it so effective. Unlike old-world celebrities, Kim Kardashian is happy to be seen as imperfect because she knows it only makes her fans love her more. She doesn't care if you think she's contradictory; her contradictions allow her to connect with fans from all walks of life, to help her sell everything from hair extensions to Balmain couture. Kim Kardashian's contouring Instagram was perfectly imperfect. It was self-obsessed, contradictory, and of course "liked" by millions and "shared" by hundreds of thousands. Few ideas or enterprises can get that meta.

For Kim to acknowledge that this perfection isn't real, that it takes dozens of products and hours of painstaking preparation to make her look "perfect," is revolutionary. Although she doesn't directly compare herself to her competition, she subconsciously shames them by inviting her fans backstage and showing them the tricks of the trade. In the future, people (and products) that take a page from Kim's book and admit their flaws, especially while competitors are hiding theirs, will have a better chance at connecting with audiences and gaining market share.

Hollywood has always been a town of transformation, where people come to forget who they are and become who they want to be. But Kim Kardashian has turned that on its head. Today, it is more important to be the person you've always been, flaws and all, and no one knows this better than Kim.

The Three Laws of Flaws

> The good of the people is the greatest law.
>
> —Marcus Tullius Cicero

Today, ideas need to be "You-centric," not "audience-centric." If this sounds like the opposite of everything you've ever heard about marketing, you're right. The principles of developing a successful idea have always been to "assess your audience and identify the white-space opportunity," but that's not enough anymore. I've done focus groups from here to Hong Kong. I've written concepts, tested concepts, and painstakingly verified *each word* in a concept, finally selecting the top-performing words and phrases that audiences have told me they like the most. The end result is a perfect ad campaign, one that reflects exactly what the consumers claim to want but rarely delivers on its promises in the end. These old approaches to marketing and product development are quickly becoming defunct. If you want to connect with Millennials, you not only have to be honest about what *you* want and show your true colors, flaws and all, but you also have to do it fearlessly.

Like all English children, my first taste of Marmite was a rite of passage. Marmite is, to say the least, an acquired taste, yet it's everywhere—spread over toast and served for breakfast. I suppose we assumed that anything that tasted that bad had to be good for you. Marmite (and its Australian cousin, Vegemite) remains polarizing—for every one person who loves the stuff there are probably a hundred who find it disgusting. It's a deeply flawed product, and its distributor, Unilever, knows it. (Ditto for Mondelez Foods Australia, makers of Vegemite.) The advertising proudly acknowledges that people love Marmite or hate it, and it gives audiences the chance to decide if the product is "heaven" or "hell." If Marmite wanted to break into the U.S. market, it could change the recipe, tone down the umami, and up the sugar levels. It might be more popular (and certainly less "flawed"), but it wouldn't be Marmite. Sincerity, authenticity, and "realness" are paramount in today's highly curated world. Love it or hate it, Marmite doesn't bend to the winds. It sticks to its original recipe and makes no apologies to the haters. As a result, it is seen as a truly authentic brand, and its fans are motivated by a sincere love of the product.

If you want to develop a fan base that is as devoted to you as some Brits are to their Marmite, then own your idea, flaws and all. Flaunt its problems and tell them in your story. Millennials are obsessed with intentions and motives; they want to know *why* you are doing something, and if that *why* fails to ring true, they will not engage. Creative ideas (and the people behind the ideas) that come from a truly passionate place, rather than being designed to please an audience, have a greater chance of success today.

Law of Flaws #1: Imperfection Is Omnipotent

> Sometimes it takes a good fall to really know where you stand.
>
> —HAYLEY WILLIAMS

Oscar season rolled around again in April 2015. I was dashing down Hollywood Boulevard toward NBC from a meeting with the CMO of a leading cosmetics brand. Walking by the Dolby Theatre, I noticed hordes of tourists and paparazzi swarming a life-sized Oscar statue slap-bang in the middle of the sidewalk. No biggie. However, on closer inspection, I realized that this particular Oscar had less than perfect posture. In fact, Oscar was on all fours, doggy style, snorting lines of blow. The message was clear; Hollywood was about to spend millions showcasing its clean-cut, bright-eyed, and beautiful stars, glowing with good health. Yet secretly some of these same stars would be following Disco Oscar's lead in the restrooms at that Sunday's glitzy award show.

Hollywood's hush-hush addiction problem is rampant, but the issue is ignored until an A-lister succumbs—the bril-

liant Philip Seymour Hoffman, for instance. I believe street
artist Plastic Jesus had a huge impact with his sculpture because
it revealed Oscar's imperfections. Forget the glitz and glamour;
the real Hollywood is tragically imperfect. The sculpture was
front-page news everywhere from the *Hollywood Reporter* to the
Daily Mail. The reason audiences found cracked-out Oscar more
interesting to discuss than the plastic and predictable perfection
of the ceremony is because everyone is suffering from perfection fatigue. We now know those glamorous girls and beautiful
boys up on the stage aren't really as perfect as they appear—and
we wish they'd stop pretending.

It's not easy to be imperfect. Most of us have absorbed
one cultural message—to strive for perfection—since birth.
But it's not always the best advice. For one thing, it can literally drive you crazy. I see it every day here in Hollywood,
whether it's the *Real Housewives of Beverly Hills* overdosing
on Restylane or the genuine A-listers who can't admit to complicated or contradictory impulses and desires in their own
lives. Second, and more important, perfection is just boring.
Audiences no longer believe you were ever perfect to begin
with, and they will ignore you (or even worse, forget you) for
underestimating their intelligence. Perfection is over. Flawed is
the new fascinating.

We were born to be real, not to be perfect.

—My shrink, Beverly Hills

At my next big charity event, I found myself sitting next to
a notoriously powerful Hollywood film producer and studio
executive. After a couple hours in his company, he reminded

me of the wife-swapping megalomaniac Henry VIII. In 1539, this king was recovering from the death of Jane Seymour and looking for his next Mrs. Tudor. An exhaustive search (as many eligible women were unwilling to consider him as a husband) identified Anne of Cleves as the perfect match.

Henry instructed Hans Holbein to paint an honest portrait of his prospective bride. Holbein caved into temptation, however, and let's just say he "photo-shopped" it a bit. Unfortunately for both artist and subject, the resulting portrait turned the master on a little too much. When the non-airbrushed Anne—acne, stocky legs, horse-face, and all—showed up at the palace, the hot-blooded Henry was less than happy. He was annoyed—to put it politely—because he was promised an unrealistically perfect bride; Anne herself had no chance against his high expectations. Anne was a savvy lady who realized that Henry was way out of her league and her life was now in danger. Instead of trying to salvage their marriage, she befriended the king, agreed to a quickie annulment, and retired early to the English countryside—head firmly intact. Fast-forward almost six hundred years, and it's the same story. Today it's not princely oil paintings but magazines, billboards, and moving pictures trying to sell us on the idea that perfection is not only a real thing but also one that can be ours if we buy the right products, embrace the right lifestyle, or do the right things. The difference is that audiences today know better. Unlike Henry, Millennials have finely tuned authenticity detectors. They're immune to unrealistic promises, whether it's the perfect body, the perfect love, or even the perfect life. While Henry VIII was captivated by this promise of perfection, today we are bored by it.[1]

Carpe Diem? Carpe Flaw!

To truly leverage the new power of imperfection, you must also act quickly, seizing opportunities to show your flaws and differentiate yourself from the misguided "perfection" of your competitors. You must leverage the natural tension that arises when audiences *are* one thing but feel pushed to be another.

In the spring of 2015 I was invited to host *Variety* magazine's YouTube superstar panel at the Four Seasons Hotel in Beverly Hills. One of my panelists was beauty blogger and YouTube sensation Bethany Mota. Bethany has almost 9 million followers and a habit of creating a female fan frenzy wherever she goes. In my study I named Bethany as one of the most influential YouTube stars in the world, and she has since appeared on the most mainstream of celebrity vehicles, ABC's *Dancing with the Stars*.

Bethany had a joint venture with clothing line Aeropostale, so I invited Scott Birnbaum, then senior vice president of marketing, to join the panel. At lunch, Scott pulled me aside and whispered, "You know, the more we Photoshop Bethany's images, the less they are liked. So we just don't Photoshop her anymore." Bethany's fans look up to her and idolize her because they know she's not perfect. She doesn't look like a movie star or a runway model. They like her *because* of her imperfections, not in spite of them, and Aeropostale celebrated her flaws.

Women today have never felt stronger or sexier. They have single-handedly redefined sexy as a state of mind and not a specific dress size.

Lena Dunham's lingerie selfie recently trended on Instagram, un-Photoshopped bod and all. On Instagram, she slammed Spanish magazine *Tentaciones* for altering her body in an image used on its cover: "It's a weird feeling to see a photo and not know if it's your own body anymore. . . . I have a long and complicated history with retouching. I wanna live in this wild world and play the game and get my work seen, and I also want to be honest about who I am and what I stand for."[2] Plus-size supermodel Tess Holliday's May 2015 *People* cover showed her similarly taking ownership of her size and her right to be happy about it. Clever ideas have to emulate these women's self-confidence and refusal to conform to old-fashioned ideals of attractiveness. Any individual, idea, or enterprise that is looking to cultivate a deeper and more lasting relationship with women has to find a way to celebrate both the product's (and the consumers') flaws and imperfections.

Flawed Ideas Will Be Forgiven

> Just because you're not perfect doesn't mean you're not beautiful.
>
> —ZAYN MALIK, FORMER MEMBER OF ONE DIRECTION

I'll never forget the night of August 31, 1997. I was staying at the Hôtel Ritz in Paris, not far from where Lady Diana and her Muslim boyfriend, Dodi Fayed, were killed in a suspicious car crash in the Pont de l'Alma tunnel. The resulting rumors that the British intelligence agency MI6 had killed Diana—because she was dating a Muslim and expecting his child—shattered the British royal family's image of perfection, cultivated throughout Queen Elizabeth II's entire reign. Now the figureheads of a new generation of royals, Prince William and Kate Middleton, are trying to play a strikingly similar perfection game. When the *Sunday Times* interviewed me on the significance of the birth of their second baby, Princess Charlotte, I had to be honest. Nobody cared. The public has grown bored with the pretense and declines to go gaga over them. Compare this to the enduring popularity of footballer David Beckham and his wife, Victoria (aka Posh Spice). Both from working-class backgrounds, their accents are flawed, they complete each other's sentences, and their actions and feelings—not to mention rumors of a split—are splayed across the tabloids for all the world to see. Yet seventeen years later we remain hooked. Nobody has to guess what's going on behind the closed doors of Posh and Becks; their imperfections are all out in the open. It's what makes them the true figureheads of Great Britain. We forgive them for everything because we love them in a way we've never been able to love the manicured remoteness of Wills and Kate. For an idea to spread, or a product to sell, it must have a uniquely strong connection with its end user.

The Science of Imperfection

I think there comes a point where you have to grow up and get over yourself, lighten up . . . and forgive.

—JENNIFER ANISTON

It's strange that we insist on trying to be "perfect," either in our personal lives or our work; after all, science proves that we distrust perfection and are turned off by attempts to copy it. Instead of loving the flawless rhythm of computer-generated beats in electronic dance music, we reject it for its lack of humanity.[3] Experiments have shown that audiences always prefer songs with random flaws—even if they are too subtle to detect on a conscious level. This feeling is so strong that sound recording software now comes with "humanizing" programs that create a slight deviation to random beats.

Psychologist Elliot Aronson's famous "Pratfall" experiment demonstrates that most men, and many women, actually like people *more* when they behave imperfectly. Aronson had volunteers listen to recordings of other people talking—on some of the tapes the person talking clumsily spilled a cup of coffee. So long as the speaker was seen as basically competent, the listeners actually liked him *more* after he spilled his drink. If the person speaking was seen as incompetent, his imperfections made him *less* likeable.[4] And this is the truth of imperfection—so long as your audience believes you are *competent*, they will forgive you and like you more for being imperfect. If your idea is not seen as being fundamentally competent, its imperfections will not be forgiven.

This hasn't stopped me from being a bit of an obsessive-compulsive perfectionist over the years. I expect the best from myself and everyone else who works with me. Ten years ago, if you asked me to explain *why* I was a perfectionist, I'd have said that only the most perfect work will stand the test of time and that only the most perfect person in their field has a chance of breaking through and being a success. Now I know that's not true. Today I'm more of an *imperfectionist*; I'm less interested in "being perfect" and more interested in challenging myself to find the imperfections that make ideas, products, and services more memorable, shareable, and compelling. After my years at Oxford and Harvard, and working at the most prestigious brands in the world, I now know perfection is not enough. In fact, most psychologists agree that perfectionism is less about improving ourselves and more about making ourselves acceptable to others[5]: that is, conforming to norms of society. And what's exciting or meaningful about that?

Before You Judge Me, Make Sure You're Perfect

You can't dictate to a woman what should make her feel sexy.

— DITA VON TEESE

I went to a Church of England school where I attended mass every morning and was raised to believe that we were created in God's image, but image is where the similarity ends. To be human is to be imperfect, and audiences today connect with human (and thus imperfect) ideas, experiences, and products. Imperfect ideas have enormous power, because they can actually shift the culture. When rapper Iggy Azalea told *Vogue* magazine that she had breast implants, I commended her honesty. When asked what she would change about her body, she didn't say she was unhappy with her frizzy hair, or tell the clichéd hot-girl story of how she was an ugly duckling at school. Instead she was honest about a real insecurity and perceived imperfection. She made global headlines not only because she got cosmetic surgery but also because she was surprisingly forthright about it. We all know that people are imperfect, but the difference between a banal and a breakthrough idea is in being loud and proud. If Iggy Azalea shouting, "I got bigger boobs!" takes us a step closer to a world where getting a boob job is as unremarkable as bleaching your hair, then bring it on.

Law of Flaws #2: Forget Might—Narcissism Makes Right

Be strong. Be confident. Be the star of your own life.

—ESTÉE LAUDER

Recently I raced into Mel's Diner on Sunset to grab a quick caffeine fix on my way to tape a segment for *Today*. Behind the counter was a middle-aged black woman who—despite the fact that it was 5:30 on a Tuesday morning—was rocking a fierce black jumpsuit, bold red lips, and the most outrageous weave I'd seen since my last BET Awards. While my handful of fellow diners were oblivious to her fierceness, I was transfixed. I once did a huge study for a global consumer packaged goods company about how black and Hispanic women view themselves; our most interesting takeaways were that Hispanic women view their beauty routine as a ritual—almost a religious process—something that creates a type of armor that gets them through the day. Black women, on the other hand, truly feel beautiful no matter what the outside world thinks, and this self-confidence is a form of immunity against other people's opinions. In fact, they feel good about their appearance regardless of whether or not men tell them they look good. Only 38 percent of black women feel more beautiful when a man tells them they are beautiful. They have a super-powered self-belief, one that their more privileged white contemporaries often lack. I stood there in the diner for a minute and thought about the extreme contrast between Mel's Madame X and the ultrathin, ultra-attractive young actresses who are a dime a dozen in Hollywood. Typically, these glamorous starlets, despite being in their physical prime, lack the extreme self-confidence of this middle-aged woman working the graveyard shift at a tourist-trap diner. I was instantly in love; she was superhot, superfierce, and frankly the most charismatic superstar in Hollywood that day, even if only in her own mind.

My dentist told me I needed a crown. I was like, "I KNOW, RIGHT?!"

—BUMPER STICKER, LOS ANGELES

If you want to get ahead, you must develop a sense of self-worth. Some might call it narcissism, but I call it self-preservation. As I write this book there are 275,812,876 pictures on Instagram hashtagged #selfie and 302,998,350 pictures hashtagged #me. That's a lot of people contemplating who they are and how they fit in the world. People hate on selfies, but like Narcissus himself, selfie takers are after more than just a pretty picture. Selfies are narcissistic in the best possible way; they allow us to experiment with personality traits we might not quite own yet in life: confidence, attractiveness, adventurousness. They allow us to imagine what being bolder, braver, and more charismatic might feel like. In doing so, selfies expose our vulnerabilities, and it's these vulnerabilities that allow us to connect with audiences.

Narcissism might well be a necessary thing. If you want your voice to be heard, then you better have the self-belief to speak up. Science backs this up; narcissists are more focused, and driven to work longer and harder, than their non-narcissistic competitors. One study of military cadets found a direct link between narcissism and leadership ability.[6] Narcissists have higher self-esteem, expect greater success and higher rewards, and are less likely to be concerned with other people's low opinions of them, which can be liberating. A solid foundation of narcissism can actually *help* build functional, happy relationships, since narcissists aren't dependent on other people for their own self-esteem.

Today, *narcissism* and *selfie* are almost interchangeable terms; any idea that wants to use narcissism to its advantage must understand what selfies *really* represent and why they are such a positive force among Millennials. Selfies feel like a guilty pleasure; yet if selfies are so superficial and the people who take them so fake, why are they so powerful? The answer is that selfies are a snapshot both of our immediate sense of ourselves—"I feel hot right now"—and our deeper truths—"but I also feel insecure and need to boost my self-esteem." Selfies are uniquely honest, showing both an ideal version of ourselves—the hottie in a little black dress—and also the flawed, imperfect side. This imperfection can be as simple as a messy bathroom backdrop that suggests a less glamorous lifestyle than we might like to project, or it can be as subtle as an exaggerated pose that hints at the deeper insecurity behind the confident pout. Selfies are a revealing form of self-examination. They expose both the obvious, literal fact and the deeper, more conflicted truth underneath it.

The First Narcissist

Narcissus has a reputation for being a self-absorbed twink who chased his own reflection in the water and fell in love with himself, at the cost of his life. Today's equivalent would be the fifteen-year-old boys lounging by their pedophile manager's infinity pool in the Hollywood Hills. It's easy to draw parallels between our obsession with selfies and the self-loving but doomed Narcissus of Greek mythology. But I think it's more complicated than that. Narcissus's mother asked a prophet, Tiresias, if her son would grow to old age. He told her, "Yes, if he never knows himself." And this is the little-known twist of the Narcissus story: he may not have been a particularly pleasant young chap, breaking hearts from here to Ithaca, but he was seeking a truth about himself, the universe, and his place in the world. Shame him if you must, but Narcissus is a more complex character than the label suggests. He was, in fact, a truth seeker, someone who wasn't satisfied with the easy pleasures of nymphs and goddesses (pity poor Echo).

Instead of blaming Millennials and Generation Z for selfie culture, let's acknowledge that humans have always been self-obsessed but once lacked the technology to bring their obsession to life on Instagram, Facebook, Snapchat, and a thousand other platforms. Selfies have existed as long as there have been humans contemplating their own sense of self and a way to record that desire. Interestingly, the one facet of narcissism that is about equally present in men and women is exhibitionism. Both sexes are likely to be vain and self-absorbed,[7] which explains why #selfies are equally #hotbitches and #himbos. Who knows what's lurking outside the frame— and who cares? If you have the self-obsession to be open about your flaws, to connect with audiences, and to create a captivating post, then that's all anyone is going to talk about. The ubiquity of selfies also points to our need for greater intimacy, spontaneity, and fun. Nobody gets this better than Millennials. Born of broken homes, armed with college degrees but limited job prospects, Millennials have few guarantees in life. So they fully live in the moment, and what could be more spontaneous than a #WIDN?

Love Yourself as Much as You Want to Be Loved

I am God's vessel. But my greatest pain in life is that I will never be able to see myself perform live.

—KANYE WEST

J.Crew enjoyed ten phenomenal years under quirky creative director Jenna Lyons, who remade the brand in her own distinctive image. The company, when she joined as a knitwear designer in 1990, was a small brand known for its predictably preppy style and popular catalogue. By 2003 the company was successful but had stagnated, so they brought in Mickey Drexler, the man behind the meteoric success of the Gap in the 1990s, to reshape the brand. Lyons and Drexler instantly clicked, and the new J.Crew was their love child.

For the next ten years, Lyons did the unimaginable: she transformed generic all-American tastes to reflect her love of pattern, texture, and color, all with her quirky, sensual style—but most importantly mixed with much love . . . for herself.[8] At the brand's peak of hipness she presented collections full of her cool-girl aesthetic, styling the models in thick black glasses and long, straight hair to look exactly like her (or, as she described it, "Little Edie goes to girl scout camp"[9]). Jenna Lyons was dope and she knew it. She was a cover star and an Instagram-friendly executive-cum-style icon in her own right. Besides, you know you've made it into the twenty-first-century old boys' club when flocks of women dress up as you for Halloween.

Lyons was narcissistic in exactly the right amount and in precisely the right way. She designed clothes that *she* wanted to wear and did it with such courage, conviction, and finesse that millions of women and men worldwide bought into her vision. The formula worked like magic for years. But in 2014 sales started slipping, and in December the brand tanked, going from a net income of $35.4 million to a reported loss of $607.8 million. An ever-competitive retail environment and a mistimed brand expansion into Japan and China were partly to blame. J.Crew also made a bad bet with its sweater order— buying too many shrunken cardigans that didn't sell and too few standard-size cardigans that became wildly popular but were impossible to find in the stores. However, the dishonesty J.Crew displayed on the shop floor with its customers was the major culprit.

In 2014 sleuthing bloggers realized that J.Crew's hugely popular Cece ballet flat—relaunched after being discontinued a year earlier—was being sold at the original price but was now being manufactured to lower standards in Brazil instead of Italy. Around the same time the brand was hit by another setback when it debuted "extreme vanity" sizing—000 (designed to appeal to its new customers in Asia but in conflict with American shoppers' evolving desire for body-positive messages). Shoppers complained that the whimsical clothes were too expensive and too impractical for school runs and company dinners. The brand made several tactical moves in the wake of these losses, and Jenna Lyons was allegedly told to stop self-promoting and to tone things down. Drexler openly acknowledged that J.Crew needed to own its mistakes and learn from them.

The company brought in the women's-wear designer from its booming sister company, Madewell, and axed numerous jobs.

Lyons drastically cut back her personal appearances. You could argue that she caved into a more conventional, less narcissistic role within J.Crew. However, I believe Jenna Lyons took an unfair dive for J.Crew; her self-promoting, self-obsessed ways made her an easy target. But it was also exactly those self-promoting, self-obsessed ways that took a forgettable brand and turned it into a global phenomenon. J.Crew was a dinosaur before Lyons came along; it was polite, genteel, eager to please, and utterly inoffensive. Lyons did exactly what Kim Kardashian would have done: remade it in her own image. She was overconfident, ignored the haters, and ultimately made it all about her—and it worked brilliantly for ten years.

There's no denying that, by 2014, Jenna Lyons was a bigger star than her brand (J.Crew and Mickey Drexler didn't get name-checked in *Girls* when Lyons played a cameo role as a magazine editor). Her honest narcissism would have reached even greater heights had the brand backed it up with consistent, reliable quality. And here's a big truth about narcissism: it has to extend into every facet of your business—and your life. I doubt Jenna Lyons was stocking up on the subpar Cece ballet flats, and if she wasn't interested in wearing them, then she and Mickey should have realized their audience wouldn't be interested in wearing them either.[10] Narcissism is a giving impulse; it stems from a passionate conviction about your ideas and your work. The problem comes if your standards are slipping and you don't notice or, even worse, don't care, then that narcissism can cross the line and you can lose your customers. Which means that you're calling your lawyers.

If you believe narcissism is a bad thing or something to be glossed over because everything should be done "in the customer's best interest," think again, because savvy audiences won't buy it and you'll be exposed as insincere. If, however, you can learn to be open about your narcissism, then your idea or organization will have the opportunity to create a genuine and honest connection with its audience. Millennials understand self-obsession better than anyone else, and they won't punish you for it—so stick to your guns and refuse to apologize for it. In the millennial economy brands need to be narcissistic enough to completely expose themselves to scrutiny. This allows audiences to make up their own minds about what they think of the brand. Being truly narcissistic is, ironically, a sign of being vulnerable—you're putting everything on the table for your audience to judge. A truly narcissistic brand understands that it can't define itself but needs to listen to how the audience defines it.

The Science of Narcissism

A little nonsense now and then, is cherished by the wisest men.

—ROALD DAHL

Let's go back to Narcissus for a moment. While the young man was mesmerized by his reflection in the pool, Echo, the nymph who truly loved him, was wasting away in a cave, literally dying of love. And here's the paradox of narcissism: love 'em or loathe 'em, narcissists are generally the winners in life. A Stanford study shows that narcissist CEOs who have "me-first" personalities and aggressive negotiating skills earn millions more than their non-narcissistic peers.[11] So, while Echo may have been kind and compassionate (and most likely passive-aggressive), by the end of the story she had become so invisible that only her voice remained—and even her voice was incapable of uttering an original thought, as she'd been cursed to only repeat the last sound she had heard. Echo was the world's first doormat.

Multiple experiments prove that the characteristics that

define narcissism—high self-esteem, focus, and drive—are powerful change agents. Most of the great business leaders, such as Virgin's Richard Branson and Google's Larry Page, and many of our pop culture icons—most famously Madonna and Kanye—easily fit into the definition of narcissistic. Even more interestingly, some research suggests that narcissism is a natural stage of human growth.

Psychologist David Elkin's adolescent egocentrism theory finds that nearly all teenagers believe they are the center of the universe and have an imaginary fan club, always watching and being impressed by their actions.[12] I find this repeatedly in my own research, when I talk to teens who religiously post reviews, vlogs, and random thoughts on YouTube, even when their videos get only a handful of likes. Despite all evidence to the contrary, they still feel like stars. Most people grow out of this phase in their mid-twenties, once they begin to have families and other more important responsibilities of their own.

This suggests something interesting about narcissism: perhaps it is a survival mechanism—one that gives teens the strength to get through the challenges of youth but fades away with the confidence of becoming an adult. In our current unsettled world of catastrophic market crashes, divided cultures, and zero employer loyalty, this survival mechanism is in fact required well into our adult lives. Narcissism gives us the confidence and self-esteem to survive and the necessary drive, resilience, and tenacity to succeed in a world full of uncertainty.

Law of Flaws #3: Creatively Contradict Yourself

Only the madman is absolutely sure.

—ROBERT ANTON WILSON

As a child, I learned the story of the king of Ithaca, Odysseus, who had left home twenty years earlier to fight in the Trojan War. His family assumed he was dead, and the world had moved on without him. Eligible bachelors had invaded his home, attempting to woo his widow, Penelope, while simultaneously downing Odysseus's impressive collection of wine. Penelope, a true romantic, wanted to remain faithful to her husband and maintain her own safety among the group of young men. So every day she promised to choose a new husband as soon as she finished her father-in-law's burial shroud; every night she carefully unpicked her day's work so that the shroud was never finished, and she held off her admirers until her husband's return.[13]

Penelope is an unforgettable character in mythology not simply because of her loyalty toward her husband but because of her skill at finessing the core contradiction of her life. She was both a vulnerable widow who didn't want to remarry and also a clever woman who had to seem *willing* to remarry in order to keep her suitors at bay and stay true to her own belief system. Her contradiction—claiming she would soon choose a husband while actively working to delay that inevitable moment—wasn't a lie so much as a well-conceived strategy. It not only allowed her the best possible outcome but also prevented the worst-case scenario. Kind of like Amber Rose, wistfully pining for Wiz Khalifa even as she fights off other suitors.

Contradiction and ambiguity are frowned upon in today's culture. We are supposed to know exactly what we want, and our words and actions are supposed to directly align with our stated ideals. If you want to lose weight, you follow Gwyneth's L.A. diet. If you want to kick your drug addiction, you follow the twelve-step program. Simple, right? Except that it's human nature to be contradictory. How many twelve-steppers tell themselves that their prescription pill habit is acceptable since their doctor OK'd it?

This oversimplified belief system has suffocated innovation and authentic interaction, especially in today's world where the highly prized Millennial and Z generations are arguably the most complex and contradictory yet. When *USA Today* asked me if the Scientology exposé documentary *Going Clear* would negatively affect Tom Cruise's summer blockbuster, *Mission Impossible: Rogue Nation*,[14] my answer was a big, resounding "Yes!" Cruise's manic jumping on Oprah's couch will go down as one of the most inauthentic events in television history, yet I believe his biggest image problem is the contradiction in his membership in the Church of Scientology. On the one hand, he has been a visible champion of his belief system. He has starred in Scientology propaganda, bromanced with controversial church leader David Miscavige, and even insisted his interviewers go through the induction process. On the other hand, when his beloved Scientology was slammed by the HBO documentary, the fifty-two-year-old actor refused to step up and defend his beliefs. Audiences are drawn toward contradictions, yet Tom Cruise refuses to acknowledge the biggest contradiction of his life—his religious beliefs. Millennial audiences know that something isn't quite what it seems with Cruise, but because he isn't willing to embrace his contradictions (and thus, in his mind, be "flawed"), they have forgotten him. If he could own up to his contradictions, or at least stop building such elaborate facades, audiences would embrace him once again. In today's world, secrets are no longer sexy; transparency is.

Like Cruise, too many corporations run a risky business and cover up their contradictions, and audiences can sense these shady facades in a heartbeat. (Remember the backlash Starbucks experienced after Howard Schultz tried to have an "open conversation" about race? The VP of operations closed down his Twitter account when attacked with his own hashtag, #Racetogether, leaving people in fits of laughter. That's how open he was!) The opportunity lies in sincere, exposed, and honest contradictions. When an enterprise or idea can identify, and even encourage, creative contradictions in any part of its infrastructure, it creates an opportunity for more authentic interactions, either between itself and its customers or within the corporation itself. Contradictions also prevent the worst-case scenario—audiences who can see straight through insincere gestures and decide to badmouth you.

The Case for Real Beauty and Real Love

> The mind is like a parachute: it works best when it is open.
>
> —THE DALAI LAMA

Unilever owns both Axe and Dove, two global brands with wildly contradictory customers, messages, and value propositions. The former uses highly sexualized advertising to suggest that women—generally portrayed as sex symbols—will forsake their bodies for body spray. Axe walks the line between titillating and "too much," and occasionally experiences the wrath of the UK's Advertising Standards Authority in its quest to prove itself as the ultimate love potion. Dove, on the other hand, has been busy rethinking the price of beauty for the past ten years. It makes feminist statements about beauty standards, champions inclusivity and inner beauty, and encourages women to reject the idea that they need to be sex symbols in the first place (all with a single hashtag). Dove's self-esteem fund works to help young girls develop a healthy body image.

At first, Unilever took some heat for its contradictory campaigns. The advocacy group Campaign for a Commercial-Free Childhood orchestrated a letter-writing campaign to slam the corporation for promoting the backward sexual politics of Axe yet claiming the moral high ground with Dove. The associate director of the CCFC, Josh Golin, explained, "Dove [is] positioning itself as a brand that cares and is trying to teach girls to resist this messaging. At the same time Unilever, in the form of Axe, is putting out some of the worst messaging there is."[15] Unilever has allowed these two contradictory campaigns to coexist without reconciling them into one corporate voice. In doing so, the brand has embraced its wildly contradictory viewpoints. This decision is brave—it exposes the parent company to charges of hypocrisy and potentially devalues the messages of both Axe and Dove. The company's contradictions don't stop here. Unilever's other products include skin-bleaching cream, sold in India, also potentially undermining Dove's body-positive image.

Unilever's contradiction is a flaw, but a powerful one, allowing for a more honest, open, and authentic connection with audiences. It is ultimately a much more honest approach to running a business than pretending your values are always perfectly aligned. And of course plenty of other companies are "guilty" of the same kind of contradiction. BET broadcasts rap and R&B videos that showcase hip-gyrating, ass-shaking women all week long, but come Sunday they switch over to gospel music, choirs and all. BET knows and accepts the contradictions of its audience; the average BET watcher may very well watch music videos on Saturday night and enjoy gospel on Sunday morning without thinking twice. We are all constantly guilty of the same "moral inconsistency" that the CCFC (among many other advocacy groups) criticizes Unilever for. Is this contradiction really hypocritical, or is it simply part of being human? Our morals aren't always in sync with what we truly want, or what we see in brand messages. A parent might be moved by Dove's empowering message and buy Dove shampoo for her young daughter while allowing her teenage son to use Axe deodorant. She probably doesn't see this as hypocritical—instead she sees herself as doing her best for her two different children. By buying products that encourage her daughter to feel good about her body and her son to feel less nervous about girls, she is empowering each of them to feel as positive about themselves as possible.

Cosmetics giant L'Oréal acquired The Body Shop in 2006. And why should this raise any hypocrisy flags? The Body Shop proudly proclaims that it never tests products on animals. L'Oréal used animal testing when it picked up The Body Shop and continued to do so until March 2013. In fact, animal rights groups have since pointed to numerous loopholes in L'Oréal's policy that would still allow animal testing if they wanted to use it.[16] The key here is to resist being judgmental; instead, remain accepting of your new bedmate's idiosyncrasies. (L'Oréal knew not to impose its own belief systems on its new acquisition, and that's what makes it a $24.5 billion company.) In 2001 fast-food giant McDonald's purchased a 33 percent stake in healthy-options champion Pret A Manger. Although the Golden Arches eventually sold its shares, the relationship worked for seven years. Once again, there is no reason why such buyouts can't work, so long as everyone involved accepts the basic contradiction of bringing two disparate ideas together. Being contradictory is about being open-minded and not defined by the rules.

Here's the power of contradiction: if we allow ourselves to acknowledge contradiction and even embrace it, without trying to justify or explain it, it leaves the door open for change, growth, and personal expansion.

Scientific Idea: Cognitive Dissonance

It's never the changes we want that change everything.

—JUNOT DÍAZ

Contradictions challenge us. We have an inbuilt defense mechanism against the anxiety that contradictory impulses cause. In 1957 psychologist Leon Festinger proposed a fascinating idea—all people hold different viewpoints about the world we live in; when these viewpoints clash, it creates a tension in our lives. In order to relieve this tension—or cognitive dissonance—and return to a state of harmony, we must compromise one of these beliefs. This compromise is done on an unconscious level, because to really believe the compromise and return to a state of sanity, we must truly believe that what we are saying is true.

Festinger proves his hypothesis with a now classic experiment. Two groups of people were given a boring task, paid either $1 or $20 for their time, and then told to explain the experiment to the next group of volunteers. The people who'd been paid a dollar claimed to be psyched about the experience, saying that they'd enjoyed it and would recommend it as well worth the next volunteer's time. The people who'd been paid

$20 were honest, saying it had been boring and they wouldn't want to do it again.

The $1 group could not explain their participation in terms of financial gain, so, in order to reconcile the cognitive dissonance (I spent two hours doing something silly for no money), they convinced themselves it had been a fun experience and therefore worth their time. Cognitive dissonance explains many of the complexities of human behavior; I'm never surprised when people claim to buy products on a specific criterion but then turn around and immediately contradict themselves when push comes to shove. We all live in a constant state of cognitive dissonance; the interesting takeaway is realizing that an idea can be incredibly powerful by providing permission to the audience to contradict themselves and live in a constant state of cognitive dissonance too.

Contradiction is as much a principle of life as it is a strategy for our ideas to spread. Contradictions captivate people. We try to be consistent, but we love the tension points that contradiction creates. Despite our best efforts we are inherently contradictory—we couldn't survive otherwise. Our inherent contradiction allows us to accept two conflicting realities at the same time (how many times have you heard of a horrific brutality in the news, and then, five minutes later, laughed happily with your friend?). Contradiction creates tension points in all facets of our lives, from how we treat others to how we shop or do our jobs. We all want to be fashionable and have fun, and we also want to be seen as valuable, trustworthy, and responsible. Yet value conflicts with style, trust is not seen as glamorous, and responsible is not seen as fun. So while we might want to be consistent, we tolerate the contradictions in our lives in order to fully live those lives.

Contradiction—like self-obsession—is a powerful force for change and innovation. It makes people challenge the status quo and helps them tap into ideas that would otherwise be outside of their comfort zone. Acknowledging your own contradictions allows you to come up with ideas that you couldn't have accepted if you were determined to be consistent. Contradiction then helps those ideas to break through and spread; it helps ideas differentiate themselves from the competition and makes them even more relevant with the consumer.

Flawed: Nobody's Perfect, Including Kim Kardashian

> Maybe our mistakes are what make our fate. Without them, what would shape our lives?
>
> —KIM KARDASHIAN

If there was ever a human illustration of cognitive dissonance, it's Kim Kardashian. She reigns above other celebrities with a television show, a gaming app, countless magazine covers, and appearances at every high-profile event. She also has 45 million followers on Twitter, 68 million on Instagram, and 42 million downloaders of her *Kim Kardashian: Hollywood* app. However, Kim is the antithesis of a "perfect" Hollywood beauty.

Nor is Kim perfect in her actions and decisions. Her wedding to NBA player Kris Humphries was called the "American Royal Wedding" and was broadcast in two parts on *E!* The star-studded event featured Kim in not one but two Vera Wang gowns and a reception menu by Wolfgang Puck. Seventy-two days later, Kim filed for divorce, citing irreconcilable differences. Humphries sought an annulment, claiming that he had been a pawn in an attempt to boost ratings for Kim's reality shows. Although she reportedly made over $2 million from the wedding, Kim insisted that she married for love but "got caught up with the hoopla. . . . [She] felt like [she] was on a fast roller coaster and couldn't get off when now [she knows she] probably should have." Since the finalization of the divorce Kim has publicly confessed that the wedding was "one of those life lessons" she had to learn.

Audiences today connect with this kind of baring, and even celebrating, of flaws and mistakes. My research shows that those who insist Kim Kardashian is a liar and faked her seventy-two-day marriage to Humphries to boost ratings also agree that an adult man who marries a celebrity (especially one whose every move is taped for a reality show) is most likely fully aware of the realities of his situation. Humphries wasn't an unwitting dupe, but Kim was a misguided romantic, and she admits it. Millennials and Gen Zers are able to understand that the perfect images plastered across media—including fairytale weddings—are not real and mistakes that are owned up to can be forgiven (everyone makes them, after all).

Today's audiences crave authenticity, and that includes *real* imperfections. While she is always dressed up and made up, Kim doesn't pretend that she's perfect. In fact, she's candid about her imperfections and uses that to her advantage by letting audiences in on the "perfection" process through her pics and videos of hairstyling sessions, makeup contouring, waist-trainers, and Spanx. She has also spoken openly about her cellulite and hairy forehead. She's made a big flaw, her extra-large ass, her biggest asset. Her "Kimoji" app, which crashed the App Store with nine thousand downloads per second when it debuted, features it prominently. I've found that those who call out her ass as ugly are two times more likely to want bigger butts themselves. Additionally, those who say she's "a crock of plastic beauty" are three times as likely to want to get a plastic surgery procedure themselves. Kim Kardashian is representative of a culture that wants to be perfect but still embraces imperfections.

What do you get when you have an honest, imperfect narcissist who accepts the internal contradictions in himself or herself? A person or idea who reflects the changing attitudes of today's world and mirrors a similarly imperfect audience seeking to make authentic connections. You get the potential to forge bonds with consumers and to break through throngs of competitors who promise perfection but don't deliver. Deliver yourself, flaws and all.

CHAPTER 6

Intimate

They slipped briskly into an intimacy from which they never recovered.

—F. SCOTT FITZGERALD

For years, actors on the silver screen have depicted love as strictly a feel-good zone—you'll know it when you feel it. However, behind the scenes, Hollywood has taught me that when it comes to generating intimacy, actions speak louder than anything. So when the *Independent* interviewed me on the shockwaves Kim Kardashian created by posting a secret recording of Taylor Swift and Kanye West on social media, I immediately understood the real reason behind Kim's actions. Swift spent months denying that she had approved contentious lyrics about herself in Kanye's song "Famous," but in the Snapchat footage, Swift can be heard describing the track as a "compliment." I questioned whether it was ethical for Kim to seemingly record a private telephone conversation without Swift knowing, or even legal for that matter. Yet I knew that it was the right move. Kim's action would generate a deeper level of love from her audience than any press release, party line, or planned interview on the feud. The path to developing intimacy today doesn't necessitate playing nicely, but it does require taking action and putting your audience first. Unlike previous generations who embraced a more romanticized notion of love, Millennials and Generation Zers need to *do* in order to *feel*. They practice yoga to feel spiritual, smoke weed to unwind, and do good in order to feel good about their contribution toward social causes. In return, they engage with individuals, ideas, and experiences that live by a similar value system.

Every Action Creates a Chain Reaction

A good example is the best sermon.

—Benjamin Franklin

Shortly after my interview with the *Independent,* I was invited to address students at the University of Cambridge in England. As an Oxford graduate, I was hesitant to cross over to the other side, but I had never visited Cambridge and was curious to experience it for myself. It seems my fears were rightfully founded, as it wasn't long before the descent into darkness began as the conversation turned to drugs, dark magic, satanic sex cults, and one of their most notorious alumni, Aleister "the Great Beast" Crowley.

In the late 1800s, Aleister Crowley earned a reputation for being the earliest Western prophet of doing as a way of feeling. Tabloids called him the "wickedest man in the world." Rock stars like the Beatles and Bowie loved him, while Satanists and pagans worshipped him. In truth, Aleister was an English philosopher, occultist, and ceremonial magician who loved writing poetry, painting, and climbing mountains. Crowley traveled the world with a burning desire to do everything—and everyone—that might help him to *feel* as much as he could, both physically and spiritually.

As a young scholar at Trinity College, Cambridge, Crowley became skeptical of his wealthy family's evangelical Christianity, noting inconsistencies in the Bible.[1] Before long, he was smoking, masturbating, and misbehaving with prostitutes.[2] Yet he still craved the kind of passion he saw as a child from his street-sermonizing father, and he was determined to find it again. Dissatisfied with college partying and sexual experimentation, he started studying magic, mysticism, and the supernatural. Crowley's first mystical experience was believed to have coincided with the first time he had sex with another man and realized that he was bisexual.[3] A year later, a serious illness led Crowley to ponder "the futility of all human endeavor," which led him to fully commit to the occult.[4] A senior member of the Golden Dawn—an organization devoted to the study and practice of the occult, metaphysics, and paranormal activities—moved in with Crowley, and within two years, this magic tutor of sorts had inducted Aleister into the habitual use of drugs and elaborate magic rituals.[5]

On his father's dime, Crowley began traveling the world, experimenting with dope, mysticism, and other religions. It wasn't long before he proclaimed himself the profit of a new religion called Thelema. The religion had only one law—"Do what thou wilt"—and was based on the belief that if you took extreme actions with enough intention and effort, you could both feel anything you wanted and attract everything you wanted, including passion, love, money, and power. Crowley created a commune called Thelema Abbey, where he and his clan started engaging in sexual magic rituals and orgies to experience truly authentic and ecstatic feeling. At the Abbey, also known as sex magic central, Crowley routinely meditated while performing oral sex on women, believing there was some magical substance in the fluid.

While on the surface Crowley's shenanigans might just sound like Russell Brand on a bender, Crowley was driven by Eastern meditational practices, which believed that conscious focus on physical action could stimulate an enlightened state. Anything could be achieved through mindfulness, and everything could be controlled with self-awareness and discipline. By channeling your energy and desire during sex, an orgasm could become a catalyst for making your dreams come true.

Crowley died seventy years ago, but his message was so powerful that he remains a favorite with hedonists, pagans, hippies, and pop stars. He graced the cover of The Beatles' album *Sgt. Pepper's Lonely Hearts Club Band*, and "Do What Thou Wilt" was inscribed on the vinyl of *Led Zeppelin III*.[6] David Bowie gave Crowley a shout-out in his song "Quicksand," and

Ozzy Osbourne released the song "Mr. Crowley,"[7] singing: "Mr. Crowley, won't you ride my white horse? Mr. Crowley, it's symbolic, of course."

Aleister Crowley wasn't so much a hedonist and a sex fiend as a person who craved feeling for feeling's sake. His real message wasn't "Do whatever the hell you want," but "If you want to feel, do. And whatever you do or feel, do it purposefully." He foreshadowed the mindset now embraced by Millennials and Generation Z. Doing what thou wilt, as a path to feeling life more deeply, is their new way of creating intimacy.

Utility with Benefits

Expect nothing. Live frugally on surprise.

—ALICE WALKER

Everyone has a gym membership in la la land. It's one of the first things I learned when I arrived in Hollywood. From A-list celebrities to out-of-work actors, *everyone* had a membership at one of the gyms. No biggie—this is the land of the body beautiful, but I couldn't help but wonder— why the obsession? I was curious to find out. So I joined one. After a few weeks of being put through my paces and abiding by some grueling workouts, I decided to use the steam room. And there, it seemed, lay my answer—as did one man's face in the lap of another. I later learned that in certain gyms, steam-room mischief was an additional benefit for those who were into that kind of thing. I don't know why I was surprised exactly, but I was. Well, maybe just a bit. The utility (of a gym) with the added benefits was a combination that was helping to create an intimate connection with its audience and assuring some serious loyalty.[8] Maybe the temple of fitness's next ads should read "get buff, get blown."

To create a truly intimate connection with your audience, ideas need to provide practical value. Millennials and Generation Zers embrace the power of living in the moment. So ideas that recognize this will have a greater success at developing a love connection. But a utility is easily replaceable if something better comes along. Therefore, providing practical value alone isn't enough. Audiences today are drawn toward products and services that provide additional and unexpected benefits. Phones don't just let you text; they also allow you to make videos and map out how to get to places. Game consoles don't just let you play games; you can also stream content and connect with other gamers. Snapchat doesn't just let you swap pics; it's also your favorite camera. Audiences today are interested in using products in the way that meets their unique needs and not necessarily in the way the product was intended to be used.[9] If you're looking to generate intimacy with your idea, be open to the fact your audience might find other uses all on its own for whatever features you consciously add—if you're lucky.

Reuse. Reduce. Recycle.

Don't reinvent the wheel, just realign it.

—ANTHONY J. D'ANGELO

While the "friends with benefits" philosophy has found its way into the marketplace, the idea itself isn't exactly new. At an after-party for the MTV Video Music Awards, I met a purple-haired pop singer from South Korea. She had a beautiful tattoo of a wheel on her lower back, which proved to be an interesting conversation starter. Turns out she was obsessed with one of the oldest inventions in the world, and kind of got me excited about it too.

The first wheels were made for potters around 3500 BCE in Mesopotamia, and it only took a few centuries before someone figured out they could also be used on chariots. Sometime between the sixth and fourth centuries BCE the wheel was put to work on the front end of the first wheelbarrow. Four centuries later, wheelbarrows appeared in China and rolled into medieval Europe, possibly via Byzantium or the Islamic world. They were pricey, but they paid for themselves in just a few days through labor saved.[10]

In the late first century CE, the Romans came up with an entirely new benefit for the wheel by creating a giant crane with a human-powered treadwheel.[11] The human-powered treadwheel crane was used until the 1900s. In addition to powering cranes, the wheel was put to use on farms and mills to pump water, churn butter, and grind grain.[12] In the 1800s, when windmills and water wheels weren't generating enough power, farm animals and even dogs kept the wheels turning. They looked a lot like the earliest treadmills developed for exercise, though it wasn't until the roaring twenties that the wealthy had dog treadmills modified so they could take long walks without leaving their grand homes.

A few decades later a cardiologist thought of yet another benefit for the treadmill. Dr. Robert A. Bruce invented the medical treadmill in 1952 to help diagnose pulmonary heart disease. Seven years later William Staub, a mechanical engineer and fitness pioneer, couldn't find a treadmill he could afford, so he designed one himself and called it the PaceMaster 600.

He sent a prototype to Dr. Kenneth H. Cooper, author of *Aerobics*, and Cooper was so impressed that he helped Staub fund and market the treadmill through his company, Aerobics Inc. Staub's invention revolutionized the fitness industry and opened the door for many more fitness-machine innovations. While the basic concept of a tread rotating on a wheel has remained the same for centuries, the way we use it continues to evolve.

Life Is a Series of Surprises

What we learn with pleasure we never forget.

—Alfred Mercier

I've never been a big fan of yellow cabs in New York City or their drivers. So when Uber, the original tech-based ride-sharing app, was launched in 2010, it was love at first sight. I could finally avoid getting snaked by someone half a block up and arrive at my destination not feeling quite so frazzled. All this from the convenience of my phone and at a significant discount compared to taxi rides.

Fast-forward to 2015 when UberPool was launched for those looking to save even more money than the riding solo service, and founders Travis Kalanick and Garrett Camp could do no wrong. The company proved it was continuing to provide real, practical value to its audience. Uber, however, overlooked one benefit that its users didn't: the potential for intimate group cab encounters. Riders began blogging and posting about unexpected meetings that led to real dates, not to mention letters-to-*Penthouse*-style hookups. *Vogue* ran an article by someone who tried UberPool as a dating app with no luck herself, but met a driver willing to tell all: "*Most* of my UberPools do that. They hook up themselves. . . . When you speak to someone for five or 10 minutes, if you are smart, then you'll know the type of person they are. But two people can write for a year and not know each other. On dating sites there's no body language. You don't look in their eyes, you don't know if they're telling a lie."[13] The shared rides also led to true love. At least one couple wrote to Uber to announce their marriage and thank the company for introducing them.

Of course, not everyone loves UberPool. Some claimed it was "creepy," while others worried that it bordered on sexual harassment.[14] Still, many compare UberPooling to a supervised blind date and say it gives you a more honest assessment of a potential match than any online profile—not to mention less pressure compared to a first date. Regardless, UberPool action skyrocketed, with millions of trips being taken in cities like Paris, New York, Los Angeles, and Austin, and 120 metric tons of CO_2 emissions being prevented in one month for the city of San Francisco alone.

While ideas often focus on addressing their customers' pain points, wants, and needs, it was Uber's audience who dictated the additional value of UberPool to *the company*. Uber understood the friends-with-benefits arrangement, and they went along with it. This open-mindedness not only strengthened the company's relationship with its audience, but it also gave them access to a whole new market.

Given the chance, audiences will come up with solutions that are as good as, or even better than, the original idea. Ideas today need to recognize the power in the unforeseen. Second-guessing, overstrategizing, or insisting on controlling the outcome might well limit the potential of success. The intimacy created through utility with benefits stems from capturing fans' hearts and minds. How we make our fans feel determines their opinions of us and their buying decisions.[15] Will Uber officially become a dating app and challenge Tinder? Who knows? What we do know, however, is that their riders will most likely follow them anywhere.

The Science of Utility with Benefits

Researchers have discovered that some unexpected benefits can be so intimate as to be life-altering. For instance, playing Tetris for as little as three consecutive minutes can weaken cravings for drugs, food, and even sex.[16] Cravings involve vividly imagining the experience of indulging in certain activities and consuming particular substances. Tetris is such a visually stimulating game that it becomes difficult to imagine anything else so vividly when you're playing it.[17]

Another study shows how virtual imaging technology could be used therapeutically to help people get over social anxiety.[18] More than a hundred different social scenarios, such as socializing at a party, approaching a stranger at an art gallery, and ordering a gin and tonic, were created. Participants were then captured on video, and their life-size images were projected on screen so they could watch themselves interacting.[19] The subjects practiced maintaining eye contact, making small talk, and testing their belief that they would freeze under these stressful circumstances. Turns out the big-screen "out-of-body" experience proved to work in the participants' favor because it felt less real than real life, and they were able move out of their comfort zones.

The system can also be tailored to address specific phobias like public speaking, intimacy, crowds, and spiders. Unsurprisingly, social phobias can lead to a host of problems, including poor work performance and difficulty establishing and maintaining close relationships.[20] Now technology is empowering people to re-pattern their brains and triumph over impairment. Companies like Beyond Care and the Virtual Reality Medical Center are designing systems that offer their audiences a bridge to embracing fear and experiencing greater intimacy,[21] arguably the best added benefits of all.

Multi-Commitment

Polygamy: An endeavor to get more out of life than there is.

—ELBERT HUBBARD

True love was always a private, one-on-one affair; at least that's what I thought before moving to la la land. Alas, like most traditions, this notion was destined to be remixed. I learned that some of Hollywood's most successful marriages were in fact open relationships in which—behind closed doors—one or both partners are allowed to "play" with others. Some celebrities, like Angelina Jolie, Tilda Swinton, and Mo'Nique, have even been brave enough to publicly admit (or imply) that they are in one. So, it was just another day at the office when I received a call from a glamorous couple who were concerned that their open marriage would be revealed to the public. They needed advice on how best to handle the situation in the event they were finally exposed by an entertainment news site. Rather than continue to dwell on my old-school notion of true love, I started researching how a similar need to fool around was also forming between audiences and ideas, and people and products.

In the light of FIFA, Toshiba, Volkswagen, and a slew of other sleazy corporations lying, cheating, and misleading the public, savvy audiences are more distrusting and less loyal than ever before. Today's consumers live in the moment. Gamers can simultaneously love Playstation and Xbox, and then jump to another console should they feel a greater love connection elsewhere. When it comes to intimacy, audiences are complex, and so are their needs and desires. Millennials and Generation Zers align with organizations that aim to authentically engage with them, for example, by demonstrating socially responsible behavior or doing something significant for people and the planet.[22] To prevent being the one-night stand, individuals (and enterprises) need to align with their audience's needs, motives, and values to maximize their chances of bonding.[23]

Ideas that recognize the fact that love and intimacy—as redefined today—are about being in bed with more than one idea, product, service, or person will have the greatest chances of success. Like it or not, the multi-commitment has arrived, so accept it and look for opportunities to use it to your advantage. Besides, it's this exact vulnerability that will generate greater intimacy and develop a deeper connection with your audience.[24]

The Many Loves of Josephine

Art is an elastic sort of love.

—JOSEPHINE BAKER

Many people blame Hollywood and our celebrity culture for promoting sexual promiscuity. While I learned that the City of Angels has its fair share of sinners, people who simultaneously loved more than one person or idea go right back to the beginning, when Eve wanted both Adam *and* the apple. While Eve got a bad rap, a twentieth-century jazz dancer named Josephine Baker turned multiple choices to her advantage, loving many men, each one as passionately as the other. She was also a star to different audiences for different reasons and raised a brood of children of many races. Born in a St. Louis ghetto in 1906 and growing up illegitimate, Josephine went on to become an international queen of song, dance, and seduction, and one of the most famous symbols of the jazz age.

Her first appearance on the Paris stage in an all-black review was highly sexual at a time when such overt displays of sexuality were far from the norm. Baker careened onstage, bodacious booty gyrating and legs flying in a mind-blowing Charleston. "Naked except for a hot pink feather between her thighs, she dry-humped and slithered around her male partner and collapsed in a torrential orgasmic spasm. She brought down the house."[25] Josephine rode the wave of Negro fever in Europe, and her intensity and daring vulnerability reached out into the audience and demanded attention and respect.

Baker soon became known as the "Ebony Venus," the "Creole Goddess," and the woman who gave "all Paris a hard-on." Thanks to artist Paul Colin, who was also one of her lovers, she became an artist's muse and the poster girl of the 1920s. She was sculpted by Alexander Calder, painted by Picasso, and called "the most sensational woman anybody ever saw" by Hemingway.[26]

Josephine loved multiple men, often at the same time. According to her lover and secretary Georges Simenon, "She test-drove every stallion in her path, from the Swedish crown prince on his swan-shaped bed to the architect Le Corbusier in a steamer stateroom bound for South America." And sex with this goddess was "body to body the whole time." Each lover felt that he was her one and only—in other words, she had a rare "gift for intimacy."[27] Dozens of men proposed marriage, including Simenon, and one year she received more than forty thousand love letters.

Josephine also sought to spread her love on both sides of the Atlantic and relate to audiences in Europe and the United States. Before her triumphant debut in Paris, she auditioned for *Shuffle Along*, the first all-black New York Broadway show, but was rejected as too dark and skinny. Ignoring the inherent prejudice of the times, Josephine refused to back down and took a job as a dresser for the show while she learned the chorus girls' routines. When a dancer left, she quickly stepped in and added her own comedic style that quickly became a box-office draw for the run of the show.[28]

But while she was only a moderate success in New York, Baker thrived in racially integrated and jazz-crazy Paris. Her provocative dances and costumes, sometimes nothing more than a skirt of feathers or bananas, let her connect with thousands of audience members. That level of intimacy paid off and she became one of the highest-paid performers in Europe and one of the most photographed women in the world. Still determined to be a success in her own country, she returned to the United States in 1936 for a starring role in the Ziegfeld Follies. Unfortunately, American audiences were still not ready to embrace a sexy and powerful black woman. Labeled a "Negro wench"[29] in the media, Josephine returned to Europe brokenhearted, but she was welcomed back into the bosom of France.

During World War II she acted as a spy for the French resistance, entertaining at embassy parties and relaying coded information in invisible ink.[30] Yet she still found time for a five-year love affair with the chief of counterintelligence while also giving some love to French ally El Glaoui, the pasha of Morocco. After the war she married her fourth husband, Jo Bouillon, and moved into an eleventh-century castle in the Dordogne. Josephine adopted twelve children from different regions and religions, naming them her Rainbow Tribe.

That marriage ended, as did her chateau life, but Josephine never gave up on sharing herself intimately with the world, and she made a remarkable comeback in her sixties. In the process, she attracted the attention of Robert Brady, a wealthy American artist. Although their relationship was platonic, they exchanged marriage vows, without clergy, in an empty church in Acapulco.[31] At age sixty-eight, with Robert still by her side, she put on a one-woman show in Paris that recounted her life story with thirty songs, twelve costume changes, and a kick-ass Charleston. She died in her sleep two days later, with rave reviews stacked high on her bed.[32]

Josephine lived fully and felt deeply and passionately about dance, music, men, and sex. Her multi-committed life sky-rocketed her to fame, won the hearts of thousands of fans, and made her the first black superstar. Throughout her life she created simultaneous intimate connections with people of all races around the world, both onstage and in her private life. That she was demonized on film in *The Josephine Baker Story* is testament to the revulsion society once felt toward intimate, multifaceted lifestyles. In truth, she was a diva ahead of her time. If she were alive today, her Gen Z fans might be virtually bed-hopping between her antics and Kim Kardashian's, and admiring both bounteous behinds.

Intimacy Redefined

You only lose what you cling to.

—BUDDHA

I'm a big believer in book smarts, but Hollywood has taught me that street smarts are of equal importance. It's why I invite some of the most prominent business leaders to USC to address my class, including John Dawson, the former CEO of Coffee Bean & Tea Leaf and current senior partner at CAA Hans Schiff. We have candid conversations about everything from politics to race to religion to work-life balance. So, in the fall of 2014, I invited Tom Speight, CEO of 2(x)ist, to be straight-up about the business of boxers.

For decades, the intimacy between underwear brand 2(x)ist and its fans was a hot and heavy affair that only men could understand—all testosterone, sheer animal intensity, and strictly no foreplay required. The company didn't shy away from its gay male following. Its advertising projected the Adonis that men either wanted to be or wanted to bed. By appealing equally to straight and gay men, 2(x)ist bridged an infamously challenging divide and became a favorite among the West Hollywood jocks, the East Village pups, and just about every tribe in between and on the scene.

2(x)ist's traditional love affair continued for twenty-four years. And then the unthinkable happened. The men's-only brand decided to give girls a try by developing a line of women's lingerie and accessories. The ladies' line was launched in the spring of 2016, just in time for the organization's twenty-fifth birthday, and to celebrate, female models turned up in boy briefs alongside the familiar ripped men on the runway.[33] The theme of the event was "evolution," and the multimedia show served not only as a retrospective of 2(x)ist's years as an innovator of men's fashion but also as an embrace of its love affair with women as a natural feature of the company's growth.[34] Creative director Jason Scarlatti explained the new relationship by telling the fashion world, "It complements the men's offering, because she is his equal."[35]

But it wasn't risk free. The company knew that misogyny was at an all-time high among gay men. In 2014 actress Rose

McGowan had made headlines by claiming, "Gay men are as misogynistic as straight men, if not more so"[36]—so there were no guarantees that the brand's loyal gay following wouldn't be turned off by its simultaneous celebration of female sexual prowess. But the move was a strategic one, led by CEO Tom Speight, who recognized the realities of today's audiences. Consumers spread their affection and attention among a variety of convictions—forget old-school ideas of brand monogamy and endless love—and enterprises and ideas must do the same. If 2(x)ist hid behind a monogamous state of mind and old-school notions of intimacy and what was considered effective emotional advertising, it would have missed a huge opportunity. At the same time, female audiences were looking beyond other women as role models, and they saw in the gay athletic man qualities they wanted to possess. Knowing this, 2(x)ist is inviting even more people into its bed and is also planning to offer its beloveds more variety. Speight envisions turning 2(x)ist into a full lifestyle brand.[37] Think Hugo Boss–meets–Kate Spade. It's a big vision for sure, but with 2(x)ist's keen grasp on multi-commitments, it's in prime position to sleep around and not feel threatened when its audience does the same.

Ultimately, 2(x)ist succeeded because it valued itself above the need for unwavering devotion from others. When you share true intimacy, you have a love connection with yourself as much as with others. You're not trying to trap your audience into being yours forever; you're letting them come to you. And shared intimacy means there's no covering up what really turns you on. Only ideas, products, services, and people that know exactly what they want—and are innovative enough to redefine norms and break down boundaries—will succeed in the marketplace of intimacy. Others will remain neatly in their boxes, to eventually be outed.

The Science of Multi-Commitment

Love is cursed by monogamy.

—KANYE WEST

As Josephine Baker proved, it's possible for us to generate intimacy with more than one person, cultural idea, or place without telling lies, keeping secrets, or feeling shame. Ideas that will connect with audiences on a deeper, more authentic emotional level will recognize this new reality.

Scientists now speculate that mating for life may not be what nature intended. *Homo sapiens* have evolved with a dual reproductive strategy that's a mix of being faithful to one mate at a time—serial monogamy—and clandestine couplings.[38] We appear to have the biochemical and genetic mechanisms that permit us to be extraordinarily flexible with commitment when it comes to intimacy and love.

Each generation's prevailing view of sexuality influences how open people are about the intimacy, as well as the love, they need. As more Millennials and Gen Zers come of age, their openness and comfort with loving multiple people and products will ultimately transform the way global audiences view relationships. Instead of exclusivity being the only acceptable option, we will increasingly accept the reality that half the marriages in America end in divorce, a clear indication that lifelong monogamy isn't working out so well.[39] Divorce rates aside, several studies have found that, in the United States, somewhere between 30 and 50 percent of married men and women are spending time in somebody else's bed.[40]

So what does this mean for products, services, and ideas? Science gives us an insight into emotional connections with people as a way of predicting emotional connections with products, services, and ideas. Anthropologist Helen Fisher believes that because casual sex occurs worldwide and is associated with a range of sociological, psychological, and biological factors, it's likely that infidelity is a core part of our primary human reproductive strategy and a survival mechanism.[41] Taking the adaptation process a step further, Millennials and Generation Zers want to marry, but they recognize that their marriages might not last a lifetime, and they certainly won't commit themselves eternally to particular ideas or products. They value the freedom and flexibility to be intimate with more than one person or brand without the old-school shame and blame of previous generations for these actions.

Multi-commitment recognizes that the greatest intimacy might not just exist between two people but among multiple partners.[42] The concept extends to loving multiple products equally and simultaneously. The rise in polyamorous unions and multiple brand loyalties illustrates an audience's ability and willingness to enter and maintain strong, simultaneous love relationships.[43] Today, consumers' capacity for intimacy isn't limited but can be developed successfully with more than one entity.

Hyperpersonalization

Attention is the rarest and purest form of generosity.

—SIMONE WEIL

Hollywood is as much a state of mind as it is a city in California—that includes its perspective on plastic surgery. I run into people every day who have undergone the knife (for better or worse) in an attempt to look like their "best" selves. From Bieber to Barbie look-alikes, I thought I'd seen it all until I accompanied my friend to a spectacular wedding anniversary party at a clifftop mansion in Malibu. The couple, named Lena and Travis, were clearly in love. In between some serious PDA sessions, I decided to ask how they met. Travis's answer somewhat surprised me. They had known each other for many years, but back then Lena wasn't really his "type." I asked what changed his mind. Apparently, Lena had a complete makeover—vaginoplasty, rhinoplasty, liposuction of her inner, outer, and anterior thigh, and a Brazilian butt lift—after which Travis fell head over heels in love with this remade woman, whisked her off to Paris in his customized private jet, and asked her to marry him. Of course she said yes. Who would refuse? They even now looked eerily similar—right down to the same teeth and bite.

Who Breaks a Butterfly upon a Wheel?

Dream more, learn more, care more, be more.

—Dolly Parton

Human beings have always been driven by the desire to hyperpersonalize, whether it's their bodies, their cars, or their lives. One person's "you be you" might be another's worst nightmare, but that's the point. If you are brave enough, you can literally rebuild yourself—in your own idealized image—from the feet up. For every wannabe Goop gal who keeps her lipo on the down-low, there's a living and breathing Barbie Doll[44] and her occasional mate, the Human Ken,[45] sharing the secrets of their dream house, extreme makeovers, and matching Corvettes with the *Daily Mail*.

The infamous Roman emperor Nero Claudius Caesar couldn't help himself either. Even by Roman standards Nero was a bit of a freak, but he had to let his flag fly. Whether it was loving up (and then murdering) his mother or playing "bride" to his Pythagorus and Doryphorus in elaborate wedding ceremonies (on his wedding night to the latter, the emperor was heard to "imitate the words and cries of maidens being deflowered"[46]), Nero was fearless about reshaping social conventions, the world, and himself to suit his needs and desires.

Nero finally met his romantic match in the winsome slave Sporos.[47] A captivating teenage boy, Sporos was rumored to have a startling resemblance to one of Nero's deceased wives, Poppaea Sabina (the easily displeased emperor had kicked his pregnant ex to death in a fit of rage). Whatever the reason, Nero fell head over heels for the tweenage tempter. He swiftly commanded that the lad be castrated (history does not record Sporos's reaction to this decree) and immediately married his new love. Nero and Sporos—now known as "Sabina," "mistress," "queen," and "lady"—lived openly as man and wife. His empress was afforded all the respect that a natural-born woman would expect, and any slut-shaming went on behind the terrifying Nero's back. This took some balls on the emperor's part; after all, the Roman empire was far from the five-hundred-year-orgy that Bob Guccionne's highbrow skin flick *Caligula* or Robert Graves's *I, Claudius* would suggest. Although many wealthy Roman men kept boys as sex toys, only Nero went so far as to turn one of them into a woman and marry her.

Alas, Nero and Sporos's love story ended as bloodily as that of their romantic descendants, Romeo and Juliet. Nero took his own life—preferring that to being murdered—in June 68 CE. His wife, still young and beautiful, sought protection in the arms of a quick succession of powerful Romans but was condemned to the gladiatorial arena by the short-lived emperor Vitellius. Rather than face humiliation in the ring, the love-lorn Sporos killed herself.

Sporos and Nero's unusual love story doesn't get the respect it deserves. Their equally hyperpersonalized descendants, such as MMA ass-kicker Fallon Fox, the Danish Girl, or Laverne Cox, have also learned that the path to hyperpersonalization can be a risky endeavor—those who dare to remake themselves in their own dream image often have to face the wrath of society and risk some unpleasant consequences. But the payoffs of hyperpersonalizing yourself are clear: feelings of greater control and an unrivaled level of intimacy.

The Beauty of Science

Character, I am sure, lies in the genes.

— TAYLOR CALDWELL

My next trip took me back to London for twenty-four hours, where I met with the management of a leading British girl group. Having conquered Europe with a string of successful hits, the girls now had their sights set on the USA and wanted to know how best to crack the market. It was during this meeting that I learned of a swanky little beauty shop called Geneu on Bond Street. The premise sounded different from the slew of beauty stores in Beverly Hills, and the pop princesses swore by their products. It was only a few doors away, so I decided to take a closer look. Responding to the personal needs of audiences, Geneu is taking intimacy to the cellular level: they've created high-tech skin care that marries a hedonistic layer of sex appeal, Dubai dollars, and rock 'n' roll panache.

Nick Rhodes of Duran Duran[48] and Professor Christopher Toumazou of Imperial College London met on a private jet flying to Venice to celebrate the notoriously hard-partying billionaire Sheik Walid's fiftieth birthday. The professor told the makeup-obsessed rock star (who famously wore the same YSL shade of pink glitter lipstick as his bride on their wedding day) about the technology he'd developed that allowed a microchip to quickly analyze specific portions of a person's genetic code. But what Dr. Toumazou saw as a way to build an artificial kidney for his son, Rhodes saw as a commercial goldmine: skin care products. By the time they landed in Dubai, the unlikely pair were partners. The new gold standard in skincare, Geneu, was the result.

The scientific skin-care company took a swab from my mouth and used a microchip to analyze the DNA obtained to determine the unique makeup of my skin and identify potential hereditary weaknesses. Geneu's testing focuses on two genomic markers that cause skin to wrinkle, sag, and blotch over time: internal antioxidant protection and collagen breakdown levels. This information was then combined with an environmental assessment to create tailor-made anti-aging serums that contain the exact dosages of antioxidants and collagen to suit my individual skin needs.

Geneu's U+microchip technology cuts out the lab altogether and provides results in-store and within thirty minutes. Rather than decoding my entire genetic code (a prohibitively expensive and time-consuming practice), the company focused on specific areas of my DNA, looking for markers of skin health that are revealed by genetic variations between one person's DNA and another's—these variations are called 16 Single Nucleotide Polymorphisms (SNPs, or "snips"). These SNPs demonstrate how well one person's skin is equipped to produce collagen, protect itself against the sun, resist inflammation, enhance its antioxidant system, and process and expel sugar.[49] If a customer has amazing collagen regeneration but lags in sugar processing, then their custom-blended product reflects this.

Clinical tests have demonstrated that Geneu's serums reduce the appearance of fine wrinkles by 30 percent in twelve weeks. Such intimacy, however, comes with a hefty price tag—£600, or about $850, for an initial consultation and two weeks' worth of product. Despite the higher price tag, customers' satisfaction ratings remain sky high for personalized products, some 50 percent higher than mass-produced products.[50]

Old Ways Won't Open New Doors

Forget the 1 percent, now it's the 0.001 percent that really counts—in other words, the percentage of genetic differentiation between one human being and any other. This magic number means that a simple saliva test can determine if one patient can metabolize a drug or if another will develop deadly—and hereditary—diseases, such as the BRCA1 strain of breast cancer. It also offers almost limitless opportunities for customizing everything from eye cream to diets to work-outs to supplement blends.[51]

While technology is taking hyperpersonalization to new heights, the move toward greater intimacy has been gathering strength for some time. The Blood Type Workout offered a personalized plan based on eight types of blood (and a healthy dose of speculation about how blood type might modify your diet) as opposed to individual DNA. The concept of individualized wellness and beauty was pushed further in 2012 when the Vampire Facial hit the mainstream after Kim Kardashian posted a bloody pic on Instagram. The VF technique spins out customers' own plasma to reinject back into their faces and to make customized beauty serums. The end result is something unique, self-reflective, self-absorbed—products that, for the first time, are literally made out of you. In today's market, intimacy through hyperpersonalization is a big opportunity for ideas. DNA tests or not, ideas need to make each member of your audience feel like they're your one and only.[52]

The Science of Hyperpersonalization

> To me the future is personalization.
>
> —MARISSA MAYER

Neuroscience and psychology shed light on why consumers behave the way they do, and leading ideas are paying attention to it. While some critics chalk it up to vanity or narcissism, hyperpersonalization makes perfect sense to our brains. In fact, one wonders why previous generations were so willing to settle for mass-marketed products considering that our brains are wired to respond most positively when we're being treated as the unique individuals we are.

Research shows that when consumers participate in the process of creating and personalizing a product, they generate a greater sense of intimacy with that product and are more likely to buy it. Their purchase preference increases regardless of whether or not they were looking to purchase that item. Science reveals that hyperpersonalization of products works by activating consumers' touch receptors and triggering sensual stimulation, even when the personalization occurs online. In fact, the power of hyperpersonalization is so potent in generating feelings of intimacy that you don't have to physically participate in creating a product for your brain's touch receptors to be turned on—just thinking about aspects of the product, including the color, size, and special features, is enough for your brain to turn on and initiate a feel-good response.[53]

Interacting with virtual objects produces more vivid mental images than reading about options or looking at photographs. The mental images create a more intimate experience for consumers, and the more engaged they are with the product or service, the more likely they are to buy it.[54] Customizing a product and being involved in the design process also gives audiences more control, which increases their feelings of psychological ownership.[55] The opportunity to have more control and the ability to express themselves through products that are made for them alone creates an emotional attachment that audiences rarely feel for products bought off the shelf. People already place a higher value on items after they own them—a phenomenon called "the endowment effect"—but when adding the emotional attachment, the value increases exponentially.[56]

CHAPTER 7

Execute

Change the game, don't let the game change you.

—MACKLEMORE

My friends think I must have known in the womb that I was different, that I would be the only one in the group to relish equally the arts and sciences, poetry and prose, the fake and the real. My parents surely intuited it, as did I from the time I was three years old. But it took a long time for me to grow into the me I ended up becoming, and to realize that my personal and mental ambidexterity were neither flaws nor without value. I had to fully experience a personal evolution in order to realize that living life on my own terms was a positive thing: indeed, the very thing that led to my success. In doing so I learned to embrace the original aspects of my own personality and use them as my strengths.

As a child growing up in Bristol, England, I was well behaved and tried to follow my parents' guidance. I wanted them to be proud of me, so I did well in school, got along with the other children, and respected the family elders. But even though I conformed on the outside, inside I felt like I didn't quite belong. It wasn't that I didn't see the need for my education or the rigors of becoming a proper British child; I just felt like I was forcing myself into a role that wasn't of my own design. I didn't much like it. So while I did what was expected, mentally I escaped to my own world. Part of that world was Hollywood, but that was really just the backdrop for the adult Jeetendr Sehdev character I would ultimately create for myself.

The character I created has as much to do with observing the world around me as it does with designing my own worldview. By understanding the dynamics that form relationships between people and between people and things, products, ideas, and ways of, well, living, I was able to create methods for answering the most fundamental questions people have about the essence of successful marketing.

Looking back across the years, I can now see that with each step and misstep, every career decision, every personal and business experience, I was creating, testing, experimenting, discarding, and refining the components of what would become JAAM. But what I initially conceived of as a framework for marketing revealed itself over time to be much more. JAAM is not only my way of looking at the world but also my way of being in the world. And in that it's a useful set of tools for breaking down creative and entrepreneurial barriers. It goes beyond the thinking-outside-the-box paradigm and encourages me and, by extension, you to create new and as yet untested structures. You can use the rules of any given game to your advantage by breaking them and then reconstructing them in the image of your own business, your own product, your own life, and your own you.

How Can You Surprise?

Let's face it: the world is increasingly global and diverse. If Hollywood has taught me one thing, it's the danger of following the pack and disappearing into a sea of sameness. Today's audiences are busting societal norms to create their own identities and don't believe it's necessary to downplay their differences to get ahead,[1] so they're drawn toward ideas and enterprises that feel the same. I've seen how Millennials march to their own drumbeat and have a tendency to tune out those who don't. The lesson: know who you are and what you believe in, and inject this personality and perspective into your product.

RULE #1: BE A DEVIANT

We're all born originals. Be your unique self, openly and unashamedly. If this means creating your own rules, like David

Bowie, go for it. If it means redefining a category, as YouTube stars like PewDiePie and Jenna Marbles redefined what it means to be a celebrity, don't hesitate. Don't let external forces— mainly, other people—define you. Just as Kim Kardashian has flaunted her pride in being Armenian in Hollywood's culture of whitewashing (not to mention her dark beauty and derriere), focus on what makes you and your ideas deviant.

RULE #2: DIVERSIFY AND INNOVATE

Don't define your world in black and white. Force yourself to experience different people, cultures, and ways of thinking, even if it makes you uncomfortable. Remember that diversity isn't only about inclusion. A group that is different in gender and race but fundamentally similar in background and experience often isn't truly diverse. Surround yourself with truly different minds, and you'll come up with the greatest set of solutions. Marriott did exactly that when it created its own media studio and brought in filmmakers to cut through the competitive clutter. So take risks and don't feel afraid to venture from your core competencies.

RULE #3: DON'T BE A COPYCAT

Copies fade fast. Don't fool yourself into believing imitation is innovation. We all have a set of unique skills and the ability to create. Live up to your potential, and your ideas will rise above the crowd to resonate with Millennials who crave originality. The big boys in the menstrual hygiene market were blindsided by the arrival of Thinx, a company that blew up every industry norm. If the norm is technical complexity, look for ways to rely on simplicity. If standards call for one size that fits all, look to customize. Aim to make a best practice even better.

RULE #4: BE BAD, AND DON'T APOLOGIZE FOR IT

Be good at being bad. It will help you break through, especially if you dare to say, think, or do something that no one else has before. Playing it safe is a dangerous game that often leads to mediocrity, so take a stand and show your confidence. This includes being true to your negative emotions. How could SpaceX get anywhere near space if no one ever got angry or upset? Be sure to continue to examine those emotions to connect with your underlying passion.[2] Your idea needs no apologies, especially if it's representative of who you are or what you believe in. Carol's Daughter did what it took to survive in a changing market. Many were angry, but Lisa Price never apologized because she had the courage of her convictions.

How Can You Be Overexposed?

If audiences suspect that transparency itself is an act, it's pointless asking what ideas, enterprises, and leaders should do to be more transparent. Many celebrities live behind contrived images in Hollywood. But these images are falling apart as audiences are exposing people for who they really are. I've learned that contrived empathy, false charm, and manufactured remorse won't get you far. Overexposing yourself by being up front will not only let others know exactly where you stand but it will also keep you from being misunderstood. Recognize what's central to you, your deepest beliefs, and values, and be clear about that identity, regardless of the blowback. There are few secrets today, and oversharing is obligatory. Never keep your audience in the dark about important issues or spin them to sound more positive, as this will only create more skepticism. Real connections are created through giving your audience limitless information, genuine empathy, and deep emotion.

RULE #1: FLAUNT IT

Believe that you've got it to flaunt it. Each one of your elements is an asset that you can capitalize on. Take a step back to examine yourself and then use your assets to make a statement about who you are and what you can offer. Share your thoughts openly so your ideas are exposed to a wide audience.[3] Socially connected Millennials are sure to notice, and Generation Zers, who are poised to be even more involved and active in charitable causes than their elder siblings,[4] will be fans. Generate buzz around yourself by talking openly about your ideas. The more people know you, the more they're likely to speak about you or your idea.[5] Madame X definitely knew her worth, and she gained immortality by flaunting it.

RULE #2: IT'S A TAKEDOWN CULTURE, SO YOU'VE GOT TO BE STRAIGHT UP

You are what you hide. If there's one thing we can learn from YouTube stars, it's that audiences relate to real and unfiltered emotions and want to know your innermost thoughts and feelings. So keep it real. Don't just share your successes but your setbacks too. The more awkward your disclosure feels, the more authentic and relatable you'll be. Telling your truth will build trust among those you want to reach. When you feel the most vulnerable and are tempted to back out, imagine the situation through another person's eyes. Remember, uncomfortable moments are human moments, so give it up.

RULE #3: DON'T COVER UP

Pretty words don't cover up ugly actions. Old-school business wisdom might insist that your image be carefully controlled, but the current moment demands the exact opposite. Don't fall for the trap of projecting an image of success like Elizabeth Holmes of Theranos. Instead, create common ground based on overexposure to build trust with others. Share information truthfully and openly. Nothing disarms naysayers more than admitting that you know you messed up and showing your audience that you respect them enough to tell them the truth. If certain information cannot legally be shared, be upfront about that too. And if you don't have an opinion yet, admit that you don't know. You have nothing to hide. Be open about your challenges—you'll generate trust and goodwill, so audiences will be more likely to give you a break in the event that you mess up.

RULE #4: CHAMPION YOU

Believe in yourself, even if no one else does. Be the biggest advocate for your ideas, and show how much you believe in them.[6] This can be a scary task, as we are conditioned to accept critique over admiration. It can also feel "wrong" to blow our own trumpet. But remember, there's a difference between feeling better than everyone else and feeling good about yourself.[7] Champion your truth and let others champion theirs. The leaders of Chick-fil-A have every right to defend their Christian beliefs, close on Sundays, and support anti-LGBT activism. Similarly, other companies have the right to skip church and donate to #Equality. Remember, don't be fazed by party lines and ideologies: your integrity shines through if you do you.

RULE #5: TESTIFY!

Stories stimulate the brain and play on emotions.[8] But don't fixate on how your story will be received by others. As long as you're expressing your truth, you'll captivate your audience through your sincerity.[9] Zola of the "hoe trip" told her own story on Twitter and allowed others to make up their own minds about it. Audiences, in turn, reinterpreted her tale and used it to address the difficulties of being a young woman today. Ideas that truly live in your heart and mind are the ones that have grown there organically.

RULE #6: KEEP IT REAL

Be exactly who you are. Long gone are the days where you could have two different selves at work and play. Thanks to social media (and a work culture that never really allows you to disconnect) private and personal lives have blurred, and savvy audiences take advantage of it. Make sure what you're saying is reflective of what you're thinking, and be recognized for who you really are, quirks and all. In doing so, your words and body language will remain aligned, and your awkwardness and anxiety will testify to your sincerity. You might not win over everyone, but at least you'll be respected.

How Can You Lead?

We live in a jaded culture. Too many leaders have said the right things to our faces, only to be caught doing all the wrong things. Millennials are looking for leaders who are "real" and have integrity, especially in their personal dealings. They may be bored with democratic leaders but get excited by *transformational* leaders. These brave women and men believe in a free exchange of ideas, often with no holds barred. They openly challenge those around them without fear of being demonized, and nearly always generate a heightened level of excitement from their fans. By standing up for what they believe in, and freely stating their opinions, they command both attention and respect. So be uncompromising, polarizing, and fear-inducing.

RULE #1: FEAR IS YOUR FRIEND

Let your fear shape your future. Like Elon Musk, use fear as a catalyst to change the rules of the game. Subject your people to constant contests of skill and innovation so they keep bringing their A-game, and pit your employees against problems, against themselves, against each other, and even against yourself in order to push them to greater accomplishment. Use fear as a reality check to make sure you take the critical steps to make things happen. Use it to help you plan in advance, and feel more prepared to achieve those results. The fear of failure is one of our greatest motivators, so embrace it. Don't play it safe when setting your goals or dilute your ideas through arguments of risk management and prevention; instead, dare them to exceed their own expectations.

RULE #2: LET YOUR PASSION SHOW

Show the world what sets your soul on fire. Manufactured charm and moral courage only last until the most upright of public figures are caught in the most downright dirty of motels. When it comes to leadership, make sure your charisma and character isn't simply a veneer. Millennials and Generation Zers understand an addiction to ambition, and they respond to those who relentlessly pursue their dreams. They understand the concept of uncompromising commitment to the cause, so don't be afraid to show yours. Let them see your emotions, your sacrifices, your excitement, and your frustration. Use your passion to intensify your focus, drive your creativity, and persevere.[10] Kathryn Bigelow might be considered a bitch, but they don't give out golden statues for congeniality.

RULE #3: DON'T COMPROMISE

If you mean it, say it. Fully commit to your perspective, know it better, and believe in it more strongly than anyone else. Never hesitate or hedge. Audiences are attracted to those who are focused, respond quickly, and speak with conviction.[11] That's what gives today's leaders their true power. Show everyone what your inner role model—your core identity and values—looks like, and use whatever time and reflection is necessary to know them beyond doubt. Embody them at all times, in all places, at all touch points.

RULE #4: BE POLARIZING

Feel free to offend. Act from your own inclinations; don't dilute your ideas to please everyone. If you are totally on board with your *why*, then you will attract the most valuable fans. Don't placate naysayers: it will weaken your stance and confuse your followers. Like Soulies do for Soul Cycle, your fans will gladly defend you and, in the process, sway neutral consumers into becoming supporters.[12] Remember, audiences today align themselves on values and feelings. Once you have won them over, they will most likely continue to believe in the moral superiority of your cause. This will let you get back to focusing on the all-important task of being you. Your emotional center determines your truth, so act bravely and with little concern for people taking sides; repeated action ultimately becomes instinct.

RULE #5: LOVE YOUR HATERS

Use your haters as your motivators. Communities come together around both love *and* hate—John Donne and CM Punk built reputations on the angry insults of their critics. So don't dismiss your haters; welcome them, and use them as a measure of engagement. Establish a "no subject is off limits" policy and include everyone.[13] Your haters could motivate your fans to defend your idea, so be sure to give them a megaphone to do so.[14] While neither your fans nor your detractors should determine your purpose (that should be all you), you can utilize open sharing to provide you with a wealth of information. Don't encourage civility if that's not your style; instead, build an environment that reflects your own personality, and let them play by your rules. Prioritize opportunities for fans and haters to exchange opinions and even insults. Don't try to silence anyone, just like you wouldn't like to be silenced.

How Can You Use Flaws?

"Nobody's perfect" is more than a throwaway statement—it's actually a fundamental truth. Audiences today understand this more than ever, and they reject the idea that there is one model of beauty, one path to success, or one right way of behaving. Instead, Millennials are drawn toward people who show their vulnerabilities and products that show their flaws. What were once characteristics that needed to be changed or improved are now celebrated as strengths. The people of Iceland are consistently ranked the happiest in the world, in large part because the culture doesn't stigmatize failure, and its citizens feel free to try things and do what they enjoy without worrying about making mistakes. They're more productive too.[15]

So don't hide your imperfections or look to "minimize" your weaknesses; this will only create an environment of distrust. Embrace them for what they are. Remember, it's your flaws that make you fascinating.

RULE #1: CHAMPION IMPERFECTION

Find the perfection in your imperfections. Lane Bryant championed "real" women and challenged society's long-held beauty standards. In the process they took down Victoria's Secret's laughable airbrushed images, which remained the dominant visual even as it reflected an increasingly smaller percentage of women. Lena Dunham has made a career from proudly owning her imperfections. If you want to attract and not alienate your audience, be proud of being imperfect. When you're real, your idea gets respect, not ridicule. You'll convey a strong sense of self-belief and individuality, but you will also differentiate yourself by sending a clear message to your audience that not only do you refuse to abide by other people's definitions of what is and isn't desirable, but you are also proud to be imperfect.

RULE #2: FIRST LOVE YOURSELF

You are the authority on your own experiences and ideas,[16] so keep building your self-esteem and don't feel afraid to show it. Refusing to be intimidated by others is a good thing, despite what others—who might well actually be intimidated— tell you. Jenna Lyons had so much self-love that she remade J.Crew in her own image, and customers fell in love with her ideas. Like Jenna, use your self-esteem to further fuel you when you encounter negativity. You are your idea's best spokesperson. If you love your idea enough, others will too.

RULE #3: BE CONTRADICTORY

The truth is that you are a combination of contradictions. Know that you're a complex being with many ideas and opinions, so resist the urge to artificially reconcile yourself and your ideas. Mind-melds are often ineffective and stressful. You're a natural-born multitasker and problem-solver, and a collection of distinct modules often at odds with each other.[17] Own your contradictions. You'll have a larger set of information to work with, and you'll potentially connect with more types of people. Unilever simultaneously manages two different products with contradictory messages: Dove appeals to real women who define beauty internally, whereas Axe appeals to real men who want the Barbie-doll hottie. As a parent company, Unilever didn't look to unify the two contradictory messages but reaped the benefits of both sides of its identity. So, use your own contradictions creatively and glean the best components of very different parts.

How Can You Be Intimate?

Long gone are old-school notions of intimacy. Despite what the celluloid world of rom-coms would have us believe, audiences are more savvy and skeptical than ever before. That's not to say that true love no longer exists, but it has a very different face. Today, audiences prize practical-mindedness as an expression of love, and if they don't get it from you, they'll seek it out from someone else. Aim to generate intimacy through action. Like Kim Kardashian, who exposed Taylor Swift with little regard for the consequences, focus on what you need to *do* in order to *feel* more fulfilled. Living by rigid definitions of love won't get you far either. Don't just look to generate intimacy over the long term, but make the current moment equally meaningful. I've learned a lot from Hollywood's definition of relationships, so be open to new ways to generate intimacy with others.

RULE #1: BE A FRIEND WITH BENEFITS

Audiences can't get enough practical value out of products, services, and ideas. Research their needs to understand how your product or idea fits into their lives. But don't stop there. Be open to providing additional benefits. Allow fans to help define your product or, in some cases, entirely redefine your idea. Act upon their feedback, suggestions, and reviews, whether you receive them directly or they're posted via social media. Uber may not be promoting the dating use of its app, but it's not restricting it either. Just as riders did with UberPool, your savvy fans may "discover" a new use for you and perhaps love you even more because you allowed them to take control.

RULE #2: OPEN YOUR MIND

Loyalty still exists; only the definition has changed. Don't demand exclusivity from others, and don't apologize for not wanting it yourself. If it means taking a big risk like 2(x)ist by batting for both teams, then go for it. Live in the moment and be fully engaged with your audiences. No experience is too small to be meaningful today, and memories can last for a second or for a lifetime. Focus on creating good times that can be uploaded, shared, and shown off. Look to improve your own life and the lives of others in as many ways as you can, and don't be afraid to show your vulnerability.

RULE #3: DO GOOD TO FEEL GOOD

You were born to make a difference in the world. Find the cause and environment that matches your values, not vice versa. If you can't find it, create your own personalized environment. Like Geneu, recognize that each customer is an individual, so get to know their unique journey so you can treat them like your one and only. Don't waste time focusing on someone else's agenda. This is your world, and these are your needs. If your sense of purpose is strong enough, you'll take the right actions to create the right outcome. Remember, if you believe it, you can achieve it.

CHAPTER 8

Conclusion

Our first and last love is self-love.

—CHRISTIAN NESTELL BOVEE

I never set out to be the world's foremost authority on celebrities; I didn't even necessarily set out to champion personal and professional authenticity. But life is a process, and my role evolved out of my willingness to take chances, to expose the double standards and hypocrisies in the people and things that make our world run. I learned not to ignore artificialities but to challenge or embrace them as the situation called for.

My life's been an amazing journey so far, but nothing like I would have guessed in secondary school. My determination to check all the right boxes kept me from seeing that success can come in many forms and in many ways, and there isn't just one way of looking at a problem or creating a breakthrough idea.

Luckily, I learned my lesson quickly during my first days in Hollywood. I began to notice that those who would have been rejected from the elite institutions I represented were prized in the City of Angels. It opened my mind to different types of people, with different attitudes and values, and quickly showed me that standing on my Oxford pedestal and looking down on others wasn't going to get me far. The vast difference between the buttoned-up British culture that I came from and the world in which I had arrived required a total reset. The same is required today for anyone who is looking to connect with Millennials and Generation Z.

Hollywood showed me that everyone dreams big and wants to succeed, but the ones who actually get ahead aren't looking for acceptance from others. While the world around them is consumed with labels such as *fat, slim, black, white, gay, straight, good,* or *bad,* the successful people ignore all that and just get on with it.

Millions of ideas, products, and services are launched every day, but only a few ultimately resonate with audiences. Despite what our culture of twelve-step plans would have you believe, there is no formula for being a game changer. There's also no pretending to be authentic. It's a zero-sum game. Celebrities who look and behave differently—often outrageously by old social norms—are getting all the attention, while the girls next door are overlooked. The smartest people in the room are falling flat, while the "nobodies" break through and succeed, beyond anyone's imagination, because they're brave enough to stand up and be themselves. The one thing you *can* count on is that if you are looking to fit into a box or are afraid to speak your mind, you will find it increasingly difficult to break through.

This book is my perspective on the world, based on my unique personal and professional experiences and what I've learned. I don't want to tell you how to think. I'm presenting my ideas and expressing my beliefs: it's up to you to take them or leave them. If you want, you can dismiss it all as Hollywood nonsense that will never work in the real world, but don't ignore this: old-school party lines are out. The Kim Kardashian Principle teaches you that empathy for yourself and standing up for what you truly believe in are essential in order to connect with audiences. This may be an alternative attitude—or aptitude to many—but it is the way I think. So once you've found your own JAAM, don't stop. Keep pushing yourself and opening your mind to different ideas, opportunities, ways of life, and ways of thinking. You're not a scientist, and you're not an artist. You're neither, you're either, and you're both.

And this is precisely why I called this book *The Kim Kardashian Principle*. The first time I saw Kim Kardashian, I wasn't blown away. She was walking into my gym, and she was, well, just another woman walking into a gym— incredibly ordinary and incredibly comfortable in her own skin. And that's the point, because the methods that Kim Kardashian has used to turn herself from ordinary woman to extraordinary symbol are taking over the world. I can be in London, Los Angeles, or Latvia, and it's clear that audiences have fundamentally changed the way they respond to symbols and celebrities, ideas and enterprises. (And *everyone* knows who Kim is.) If you want to successfully speak to those audiences and get your products to resonate, you need to change too. But in order to do that you have to be willing to break down convention and old ways of thinking and doing. You have to focus not on judging how others live their lives or have created their images, but on how you want to live and on what you want to create. Because of the Kim Kardashian Principle, there is more opportunity than ever to create some mindblowing, world-changing ideas. What will your idea be?

Notes

Chapter 2: Surprise

1. "Deviant," *Merriam-Webster*, http://www.merriam-webster.com /dictionary/deviant.

2. Jaana Juvonen and Adriana Galván, "Bullying as a Means to Foster Compliance," https://people.healthsciences.ucla.edu/institution/publica tion-download?publication_id=1898322.

3. Sally Raskoff, "Suicide: The Need for Social Solidarity," *Everyday Sociology Blog*, October 18, 2010, http://www.everydaysociologyblog .com/2010/10/suicide-the-need-for-social-solidarity.html.

4. "History of the Prison System," The Howard League for Penal Reform, http://howardleague.org/history-of-the-penal-system/.

5. Christopher Klein, "Before Salem, the First American Witch Hunt," *History*, October 31, 2012, http://www.history.com/news/before -salem-the-first-american-witch-hunt.

6. Alex Ross, "Berlin Story: How the Germans Invented Gay Rights— More than a Century Ago," *New Yorker*, January 26, 2015, http://www .newyorker.com/magazine/2015/01/26/berlin-story.

7. "Victims of the Nazi Era: Nazi Racial Ideology," *Holocaust Encyclopedia*, United States Holocaust Memorial Museum, last updated July 2, 2016, http://www.ushmm.org/wlc/en/article.php?ModuleId=10007457.

8. Tara Culp-Ressler, "Forcing Kids to Stick to Gender Roles Can Actually Be Harmful to Their Health," *ThinkProgress*, August 7, 2014, http://thinkprogress.org/health/2014/08/07/3468380/gender-roles-health-risks/.

9. Mona Chalabi, "How Anti-Muslim Are Americans? Data Points to Extent of Islamophobia," *The Guardian*, December 8, 2015, http://www.theguardian.com/us-news/2015/dec/08/muslims-us-islam-islamophobia-data-polls.

10. Nicole Plumridge, "Solomon Asch's Experiment on Conformity," Psych.com, August 28, 2013, http://psychminds.com/solomon-aschs-experiment-conformity/.

11. Henry Blodget, "Bernie Madoff's Victims: The List," *Business Insider*, December 23, 2008, http://www.businessinsider.com/2008/12/bernie-madoff-hosed-client-list.

12. Kenji Yoshino and Christie Smith, "Fear of Being Different Stifles Talent, *Harvard Business Review*, March 2014, https://hbr.org/2014/03/fear-of-being-different-stifles-talent.

13. Radhika Sanghani, "Instagram Deletes Woman's Period Photos—But Her Response Is Amazing," *Telegraph*, March 30, 2015, http://www.telegraph.co.uk/women/life/instagram-deletes-womans-period-photos-but-her-response-is-amazing/.

14. Kira Cochrane, "The Fourth Wave of Feminism: Meet the Rebel Women," *The Guardian*, December 10, 2013, http://www.theguardian.com/world/2013/dec/10/fourth-wave-feminism-rebel-women.

15. Jillian Berman, "Even Companies That Sell Tampons Are Run by Men," *Huffington Post*, July 22, 2014, http://www.huffingtonpost.com/2014/07/21/women-companies_n_5563256.html?utm_hp_ref=black-voices&ir=Black+Voices.

16. Rachel Krantz, "THINX Underwear Ads on NYC Subway Are Up—But the Company Has Another Big Announcement," *Bustle*, November 9, 2015, http://www.bustle.com/articles/122564-thinx-underwear-ads-on-nyc-subway-are-up-but-the-company-has-another-big-announcement.

17. Sophie Kleeman, "3 Months Later, Here's How These Magic Period Panties Are Selling," Mic.com, August 14, 2015, https://mic.com/articles/123912/3-months-later-here-s-how-these-magic-period-panties-are-selling#.XdYfmhEkf.

18. J. R. Thorpe, "The History of the Tampon—Because They Haven't Always Been for Periods," *Bustle*, November 19, 2015, http://www .bustle.com/articles/124929-the-history-of-the-tampon-because -they-havent-always-been-for-periods.

19. T. L. Stanley, "These Ads for Period Underwear Aren't Too Risqué for the NYC Subway after All," *Adweek*, October 23, 2015, http:// www.adweek.com/adfreak/these-ads-period-underwear-arent-too -risqu-run-nyc-subway-after-all-167729.

20. Krantz, "THINX Underwear Ads."

21. "We Bleed for Feminine Empowerment," shethinx.com, http://www .shethinx.com/pages/power-of-the-purchase/.

22. Ruth Howarth and Charlie Edge, "Does Our Period Blood Protest Make You Feel Uncomfortable? That's the Point," *Independent*, November 10, 2015, http://www.independent.co.uk/voices/we-protested -outside-parliament-while-bleeding-without-tampons-because -a6728456.html.

23. Stephen Morris, "UK Company to Introduce 'Period Policy' for Female Staff," *The Guardian*, March 2, 2016, http://www.theguardian .com/lifeandstyle/2016/mar/02/uk-company-introduce-period -policy-female-staff.

24. Natalie Roterman, "President Obama Talks Tampon Tax and Periods with Ingrid Nilsen," *Latin Times*, January 20, 2016, http://www .latintimes.com/pulse/president-obama-talks-tampon-tax-and-peri ods-ingrid-nilsen-365228.

25. Gina Grillo, "Diverse Workforces Are More Innovative," *The Guardian*, March 27, 2014, http://www.theguardian.com/media-network/media -network-blog/2014/mar/27/diversity-innovation-startups-fortune -500-companies.

26. Daniel Tencer, "Forbes Survey: Workplace Diversity Key to Innovation," *Huffington Post Canada*, July 29, 2011, http://www.huffingtonpost .ca/2011/07/29/workplace-diversity-innovation_n_913214.html.

27. Beth Comstock, "Innovation Springs from the Unexpected Meeting of Minds," *Harvard Business Review*, March 9, 2016, https://hbr.org /2016/03/innovation-springs-from-the-unexpected-meeting-of -minds.

28. Jodi Goldstein, Bruce Evans, and Bridgitt Evans, "Different Perspectives Come Together to Form Better Ideas," Harvard Innovation Labs,

November 11, 2015, https://i-lab.harvard.edu/news/different-pers pectives-come-together-to-form-better-ideas/.

29. Gillian B. White, "The Weakening Definition of 'Diversity,'" *The Atlantic*, May 13, 2015, http://www.theatlantic.com/business/archive /2015/05/the-weakening-definition-of-diversity/393080/.

30. Brett Patten, "Hotel Sales Formula That Goes against All Conventional Wisdom," eHotelier, August 29, 2013, http://ehotelier.com /news/2013/08/29/hotel-sales-formula-that-goes-against-all -conventional-wisdom/.

31. "JW Marriott Hotels & Resorts and Marriott Content Studio Take 'Two Bellmen' Film Series to Dubai," *Marriott News Center*, November 10, 2015, news.marriott.com/2015/11/jw-marriott-hotel-resorts -and-marriott-content-studio-takes-two-bellmen-film-series-to -dubai.html.

32. John Plunkett, "TV Advertising Skipped by 86% of Viewers," *The Guardian*, August 24, 2010, http://www.theguardian.com/media/2010 /aug/24/tv-advertising.

33. Samantha Shankman, "The First Film from Marriott's In-House Studio Is about Bellhops and Parkour," *Skift*, February 10, 2015, https:// skift.com/2015/02/10/the-first-film-from-marriotts-in-house -studio-is-about-bellhops-and-parkour/.

34. Richard Verrier, "JW Marriott Branches Out into Filmmaking to Draw Younger Travelers," *Los Angeles Times*, April 10, 2015, http:// www.latimes.com/entertainment/envelope/cotown/la-et-ct-marri ott-hotels-filmmaking-20150410-story.html.

35. "JW Marriott Hotels & Resorts and Marriott Content Studio Debut Short Film 'Two Bellmen Two,'" *Marriott News Center*, February 5, 2016, http://news.marriott.com/2016/02/jw-marriott-hotels-resorts -and-marriott-content-studio-debut-short-film-two-bellen-two .html.

36. Jasjit Singh and Lee Fleming, "Lone Inventors as Sources of Breakthroughs: Myth or Reality?" *Management Science* 56, no. 1 (January 2010): 41–56.

37. Cedric Herring, "Does Diversity Pay? Race, Gender, and the Business Case for Diversity," *American Sociological Review* 74 (April 2009): 208–24.

38. Phillips, "How Diversity Makes Us Smarter."

39. Laura Stampler, "A Brief History of Shia LaBeouf Copying the Work of Others," *Time*, February 10, 2014, http://time.com/6094/shia -labeouf-plagiarism-scandal/.

40. Ned Ehrbar, "Shia LaBeouf Slaps Fan during Performance Art Elevator Stunt," *CBS News*, February 22, 2016, http://www.cbsnews .com/news/shia-labeouf-slaps-fan-elevator-stunt/.

41. Alison Boshoff, "£1,400-a-day Drugs Binges. Thousands of Women. All in the Knowledge That He Was HIV Positive: Decadence That Destroyed Prince of Hollywood Charlie Sheen," *Daily Mail*, November 18, 2015, http://www.dailymail.co.uk/tvshowbiz/article-3322969 /Charlie-Sheen-s-1-400-drug-binges-knew-HIV-positive.html.

42. Jose Paglieri, "Fiat Is 'Winning' with Charlie Sheen Ad," *CNN Money*, March 2, 2012, money.cnn.com/2012/03/02/autos/charlie_sheen _fiat/.

43. Liz McNeil and Aurelie Corinthios, "Charlie Sheen in Talks to Write Tell-All Memoir: Source," *Entertainment Weekly*, November 20, 2015, http://www.ew.com/article/2015/11/20/charlie-sheen-talks-write -tell-all-memoir.

44. David Hochman, "Playboy Interview: Gary Oldman," *Playboy*, June 24, 2014, http://www.playboy.com/articles/gary-oldman-play boy-interview?page=4.

45. Gen, "Black Women Are Regaining Market Share in the Beauty Supply Industry," *Black Girl with Long Hair*, September 11, 2014, http:// blackgirllonghair.com/2014/09/the-ny-times-reports-that-black -women-are-regaining-market-share-in-the-beauty-supply -industry/.

46. Tamara Warren, "Oprah Winfrey Decoded: Makings of a Multimedia Master," *Black Enterprise*, May 25, 2011, http://www.blackenterprise .com/lifestyle/oprah-winfrey-decoded/.

47. Tamara E. Holmes, "Natural Hair Is Big Business for Black Entrepreneurs," *Black Enterprise*, October 4, 2013 http://www.blackenter prise.com/lifestyle/natural-hair-is-big-business-for-black-entrepre neurs/2/.

48. "Natural Hair: Carol's Daughter Adds New Faces—Solange, Cassie, and Selita," Business Coach for Spiritual Entrepreneurs with Kristi S.,

April 15, 2011, https://enjoyingthejourneys.com/2011/04/15/natural
-hair-carols-daughter-adds-new-facessolange-cassie-and-selita/.

49. Quoted in Karen Grigsby Bates, "A Black Cosmetic Company Sells,
Or Sells Out?" *CodeSwitch*, NPR, October 24, 2014, http://www.npr
.org/sections/codeswitch/2014/10/24/358263731/a-black-cosmetic
-company-sells-or-sells-out.

50. Panama Jackson, "Represent, Represent: Carol's Daughter," *Very
Smart Brothas*, April 20, 2011, http://verysmartbrothas.com/carols
-daughter-campaign-lisa-price/.

51. Nowile Rooks, quoted in Bates, "A Black Cosmetic Company Sells,
or Sells Out?"

52. Chavie Lieber, "Is Carol's Daughter Selling Out or Growing Up?"
Racked, November 17, 2014, at http://www.racked.com/2014/11/17
/7568691/carols-daughter-loreal-lisa-price.

53. Ibid.

54. PR Newswire, Carol's Daughter, August 27, 2015, http://www
.multivu.com/players/English/7599051-carol-s-daughter-bornand
made-campaign/.

55. Vanessa Grigoriadis, "Kim Kardashian: American Woman," *Rolling
Stone*, July 27, 2015, http://www.rollingstone.com/culture/features
/kim-kardashian-american-woman-cover-story-20150727#ixzz
47WkvsqkT.

56. Ibid.

Chapter 3: Expose

1. Jason Farago, "Who Was the Mysterious Madame X in Sargent's Portrait?" BBC, January 2, 2015, http://www.bbc.com/culture/story
/20141222-who-was-the-mysterious-madame-x.

2. Jonathan Jones, "Madame XXX," *The Guardian*, February 1, 2006,
http://www.theguardian.com/culture/2006/feb/01/3.

3. "PewDiePie," *StatSheep*, http://www.statsheep.com/pewdiepie.

4. Tom Gerencer, "PewDiePie Net Worth," *Money Nation*, January 2,
2016, http://moneynation.com/pewdiepie-net-worth/.

5. Desiree Murphy, "Gwen Stefani Can't Stop Loving on Blake Shelton
and It's Insanely Sweet," *ET Online*, March 31, 2016, http://www
.etonline.com/news/185723_gwen_stefani_cannot_stop_loving
_on_blake_shelton_and_its_insanely_sweet/.

6. Listener RayDeo, commenting on Jean Fain, "Is the Weight Watchers-Oprah Winfrey Partnership Good for Dieters?" NPR, November 9, 2015, http://www.npr.org/sections/thesalt/2015/11/09/455322454/is-the-weight-watchers-oprah-winfrey-partnership-good-for-dieters.

7. Gina Rivieccio, "Celebrities Sharing Their Abortion Stories: Contrived or Meaningful?" *Culled Culture*, April 16, 2015, http://www.culledculture.com/celebrities-sharing-their-abortion-stories-contrived-or-meaningful/.

8. Jenna Marbles, "How to Trick People into Thinking You're Good Looking," YouTube, July 9, 2010, https://www.youtube.com/watch?v=OYpwAtnywTk.

9. Jeetendr Sehdev, "Celebrity & the YouTube Generation," JAAM 2015 study.

10. Jordan Gerard, "I Hate Joey Graceffa," YouTube, March 2, 2013, https://www.youtube.com/watch?v=egOHktOQvq0.

11. KSI, "KSI Reacting to Teens Reacting to KSIOlajidebt," YouTube, August 10, 2013, https://www.youtube.com/watch?v=wCTWC5opFeU.

12. Vlad Savov, "A Fine Mess: How Not to Assert Your Copyright in the YouTube Age," *The Verge*, February 6, 2016, http://www.theverge.com/2016/2/6/10926230/fine-bros-react-world-controversy

13. Sehdev, "Celebrity."

14. NextShark editorial staff, "How a College Dropout Became the Youngest Self-Made Female Billionaire in the World," *NextShark*, September 25, 2015, http://nextshark.com/elizabeth-holmes-theranos/.

15. Kevin Loria, "America's Youngest Female Billionaire Explains Where Her Transformative Idea Came From," *Business Insider*, November 18, 2014, http://www.businessinsider.com/why-elizabeth-holmes-started-theranos-2014-11.

16. Kevin Loria, "Scientists Are Skeptical about the Secret Blood Test That Has Made Elizabeth Holmes a Billionaire," *Business Insider*, April 25, 2015, http://www.businessinsider.com/science-of-elizabeth-holmes-theranos-2015-4.

17. Kimberly Weisul, "How Playing the Long Game Made Elizabeth Holmes a Billionaire," *Inc.*, September 3, 2016, http://www.inc.com/magazine/201510/kimberly-weisul/the-longest-game.html.

18. Ibid.

19. Full text of CMS letter available at https://cdn2.vox-cdn.com/uploads /chorus_asset/file/5969923/Theranos_Inc_Cover_Letter_01-25 -2016.0.pdf.

20. John P. A. Ioannidis, "Stealth Research: Is Biomedical Innovation Happening Outside the Peer-Reviewed Literature?" *JAMA*, February 17, 2015, http://jama.jamanetwork.com/article.aspx?articleid =2110977.

21. Jean-Louis Gassée, "Theranos Trouble: A First Person Account," *Monday Note*, October 18, 2015, http://www.mondaynote.com/2015/10 /18/theranos-trouble-a-first-person-account/.

22. Lydia Ramsey, "Some People Who've Tried Theranos' Tests Have Gotten Widely Inaccurate Results," *Tech Insider*, October 15, 2015, http://www.techinsider.io/report-finds-theranos-overshot-results -2015-10.

23. Sarah Buhr, "Theranos Founder Elizabeth Holmes Attempts to Clear Up the Bad Blood with WSJ," *TechCrunch*, October 21, 2015, http:// techcrunch.com/2015/10/21/theranos-founder-elizabeth-holmes -attempts-to-clear-up-the-bad-blood-with-wsj/.

24. Rheana Murray, "Subway Commercial Spokesman Jared Fogle Marks 15 Years of Turkey Subs and Keeping the Weight Off," *New York Daily News*, June 9, 2013, http://www.nydailynews.com/life-style/health /jared-subway-guy-marks-15-years-turkey-subs-article-1.1365511.

25. Christina Littlefield and Ryan Parker, "The Subway Guy: How Jared Fogle Went from Overweight Student to Cultural Icon," *Los Angeles Times*, July 7, 2015, http://www.latimes.com/business/la-fi-jared -fogle-subway-20150707-htmlstory.html.

26. Alicia Jessop, "Subway's Partnership with Michael Phelps Brings the Brand Large-Scale Exposure," *Forbes*, July 17, 2012, http://www.forbes .com/sites/aliciajessop/2012/07/17/subways-partnership-with-michael -phelps-brings-the-brand-large-scale-exposure/#29675077205a.

27. Murray, "Subway Commercial Spokesman."

28. Maureen Morrison, "Study: Subway's Advertising Most Effective in Restaurant Space," *AdAge*, October 16, 2013, http://adage.com/article /news/study-subway-s-advertising-effective/244761/.

29. Greg Margason and Kendall Downing, "Executive Director of Jared Foundation Arrested on Child Pornography, Exploitation Charges," Fox59.com, April 29, 2015, http://fox59.com/2015/04/29/executive

-director-of-jared-foundation-arrested-on-child-pornography
-charges/.

30. "FBI Informant Shares Lurid Details of Jared Fogle Recordings," CBS
News, October 29, 2015, http://www.cbsnews.com/news/fbi-infor
mant-shares-lurid-details-of-jared-fogle-secret-recordings/.

31. Frazier Tharpe, "Zola's Twitter Tale of Strippers in Florida Is Easily
the Wildest Thing You'll Read All Week," *Complex*, October 28,
2015, http://www.complex.com/pop-culture/2015/10/zola-twitter
-insane-epic-story.

32. Caitlin Dewey, "The True Story behind 'Zola,' the Epic Twitter Story
Too Crazy to Be Real," *Washington Post*, November 2, 2015, https://
www.washingtonpost.com/news/the-intersect/wp/2015/11/02/the
-true-story-behind-zola-the-epic-twitter-story-too-crazy-to-be-real/.

33. Associated Press Reporter and Chris Pleasance, "Disgraced Former
Subway Pitchman Jared Fogle Sues the Director of His Charity—Who
Was also Arrested on Child Porn Charges—Over $191,000 Unpaid
Personal Loan," *Daily Mail*, August 31, 2015, http://www.dailymail
.co.uk/news/article-3217485/Disgraced-former-Subway-pitchman
-Jared-Fogle-sues-director-charity-arrested-child-porn-charges-191
-000-unpaid-personal-loan.html.

34. Grant Barrett, "A Wordnado of Words in 2013," *New York Times*,
Dec. 21, 2013. Available at http://www.nytimes.com/2013/12/22
/opinion/sunday/a-wordnado-of-words-in-2013.html.

35. "Bitchy Resting Face," YouTube, https://www.youtube.com/watch?v
=3v98CPXNiSk.

36. "Resting Bitch Face," Know Your Meme, http://knowyourmeme
.com/memes/resting-bitch-face.

37. Caitlin Gibson, "Scientists Have Discovered What Causes Resting
Bitch Face," *Washington Post*, Feb. 2, 2016. Available at https://www
.washingtonpost.com/news/arts-and-entertainment/wp/2016/02/02
/scientists-have-discovered-the-source-of-your-resting-bitch-face/.

38. Gibson, "Scientists Have Discovered What Causes Resting Bitch Face."

39. Ibid.

40. The Coca-Cola Company, "Mission, Vision & Values," available at
http://www.coca-colacompany.com/our-company/mission-vision
-values/.

41. Patrick Kulp, "'Share a Coke with Obesity' Campaign Trolls Coke

into Creating an Undermining Label," *Mashable*, September 19, 2015, http://mashable.com/2015/09/19/share-a-coke-with-obesity-health -group-trolls-soda-giant-with-customized-label/#h3Jlwpt7xqq4.

42. Dodai Stewart, " 'Honest' Version of Coca Cola's Anti-Obesity Ad Is Actually a Scary Truth Bomb," *Jezebel*, January 1, 2017, http://jezebel .com/5976720/honest-version-of-coca-colas-anti-obesity-ad-is -actually-a-scary-truth-bomb.

43. Billboard staff, "Mountain Dew Introduces Creepy PuppyMon- keyBaby in Super Bowl Ad," *Billboard*, February 3, 2016, http://www .billboard.com/articles/news/super-bowl/6866063/mountain-dew -puppy-monkey-baby-super-bowl-ad.

44. Josh Israel, "Why Chick-Fil-A's Anti-LGBT Giving Is Still a Problem," *ThinkProgress*, February 2, 2016. Available at http://thinkprogress.org /lgbt/2016/02/02/3745345/chick-fil-a-still-anti-gay/.

45. Hayley Peterson, "How Chick-fil-A's Restaurants Sell Three Times as Much as KFC," *Business Insider*, August 5, 2015, http://www .businessinsider.com/how-chick-fil-a-is-dominating-fast-food -2015-8.

46. Diana I. Tamir and Jason P. Mitchell, "Disclosing Information about the Self Is Intrinsically Rewarding," *Proceedings of the National Academy of Sciences* 109, no. 21 (May 22, 2012): 8038–8043, doi: 10.1073/ pnas.1202129109.

47. L. Reinecke and S. Trepte, "Authenticity and Well-Being on Social Network Sites: A Two-Wave Longitudinal Study on the Effects of On- line Authenticity and the Positivity Bias in SNS Communication," *Computers in Human Behavior* 30 (2014): 95–102.

48. Dan Avery, "Madonna Will Cut the Bitch Who Released Her New Album," *NewNowNext*, December 18, 2014, http://www.newnownext .com/madonna-will-cut-the-bitch-who-leaked-her-new-album/12 /2014/.

49. "Kim Kardashian Writes Essay on Empowerment after Backlash for NSFW Selfie," *Just Jared*, March 8, 2016, http://www.justjared.com /2016/03/08/kim-kardashian-writes-essay-on-empowerment-after -backlash-for-nsfw-selfie/?trackback=tsmclip.

50. Scott Tenorman, "Kim Talks about Her Sex Tape," Metro.co.uk, Jan- uary 30, 2008, http://metro.co.uk/2008/01/30/kim-talks-about-her -sex-tape-200417/.

51. Quoted in Lisa Leff, "Kim Kardashian Says Sexy Selfies Can Be Empowering," *AP The Big Story*, July 1, 2015, http://bigstory.ap .org/article/f1bc5ac8b1394141a7a11c80d3894112/kim-kardashian -says-sexy-selfies-can-be-empowering.

52. Quoted in Leff, "Kim Kardashian Says."

Chapter 4: Lead

1. Jeffrey Pfeffer, "Getting beyond the BS of Leadership Literature," *McKinsey Quarterly*, January 2016, www.mckinsey.com/global-themes /leadership/getting-beyond-the-bs-of-leadership-literature.

2. Trevor Timm, "I Hate to Say It, but Sometimes Donald Trump Speaks the Truth," *The Guardian*, August 20, 2015, http://www.theguardian .com/commentisfree/2015/aug/20/donald-trump-republican-truthteller.

3. Ibid.

4. Andrew Buncombe, "Donald Trump and Ted Cruz Engage in Late Night Twitter War as Campaign Descends to 'Gutter Politics,'" *Independent*, March 24, 2016, http://www.independent.co.uk/news/world /americas/us-elections/donald-trump-and-ted-cruz-engage-in-late -night-twitter-war-as-campaign-descends-to-gutter-politics-a694 9876.html.

5. Sally Holmes, "Why Is Jennifer Aniston Always Pregnant?" *Elle*, September 24, 2015, http://www.elle.com/culture/celebrities/a30677 /jennifer-aniston-pregnant/.

6. Mary C. Lamia, "The Complexity of Fear," *Psychology Today*, December 15, 2011, https://www.psychologytoday.com/blog/intense-emo tions-and-strong-feelings/201112/the-complexity-fear.

7. Gerald Flurry, "Churchill's Warning for Today," *Trumpet*, March– April 2005, https://www.thetrumpet.com/article/1332.24.71.0/world /world-war-ii/churchills-warning-for-today.

8. Ibid.

9. Nadège Mougel, "World War I Casualties," trans. Julie Gratz, *Reperes*, 2011, http://www.centre-robert-schuman.org/userfiles/files/REPE RES%20%E2%80%93%20module%201-1-1%20-%20explana tory%20notes%20%E2%80%93%20World%20War%20I%20casual ties%20%E2%80%93%20EN.pdf.

10. Pankaj Mishra, "The Last Dalai Lama?" *New York Times Magazine*, December 1, 2015, http://www.nytimes.com/2015/12/06/magazine

/the-last-dalai-lama.html?rref=collection%2Ftimestopic%2FDalai%20Lama&action=click&contentCollection=timestopics&region=stream&module=stream_unit&version=latest&contentPlacement=1&pgtype=collection&_r=0.

11. Colin Freeman, "Dalai Lama Says That Any Female Successor Would Have to Be 'Attractive,'" *Telegraph*, September 23, 2015, www.telegraph.co.uk/news/worldnews/asia/tibet/11885441/Dalai-Lama-says-that-any-female-successor-would-have-to-be-attractive.html.

12. Mishra, "The Last Dali Lama?"

13. Kia Makarechi, "5 Things Elon Musk Fears," *Vanity Fair*, May 14, 2015, http://www.vanityfair.com/news/2015/05/5-elon-musk-fears.

14. Meghan Daum, "Elon Musk Wants to Change How (and Where) Humans Live," *Vogue*, September 21, 2015.

15. Shane Snow, "Steve Jobs's and Elon Musk's Counterintuitive Leadership Traits," *Fast Company*, June 4, 2015, http://www.fastcompany.com/3046916/lessons-learned/elon-musks-leadership-traits.

16. Ibid.

17. Max Chafin, "Elon Musk's Guide to the Galaxy," *Inc.*, October 1, 2010, http://www.inc.com/magazine/20101001/elon-musks-guide-to-the-galaxy.html.

18. Ross Andersen, "Exodus," *Aeon*, September 30, 2014, https://aeon.co/essays/elon-musk-puts-his-case-for-a-multi-planet-civilisation.

19. Tony Reichhardt, "Telepresence and Virtual Reality May Be the Keys to Mars Exploration," *Air & Space Magazine*, December 2015, http://www.airspacemag.com/space/telepresence-space-mars-180957306/?no-ist.

20. Harvey Milkman, "The Joy of Fear—Why Halloween?" *Psychology Today*, October 25, 2009, https://www.psychologytoday.com/blog/better-dope/200910/the-joy-fear-why-halloween.

21. Heather Hatfield, "Extreme Sports: What's the Appeal?" *WebMD*, 2006, 4–5, http://www.webmd.com/fitness-exercise/extreme-sports-whats-appeal?page=4.

22. Alice Park, "Why We Take Risks—It's the Dopamine," *Time*, December 30, 2008, http://content.time.com/time/health/article/0,8599,1869106,00.html.

23. "The Fun Side of Fear: Thrill Seekers," Goose Bumps! The Science of Fear, http://www.fearexhibit.org/fun_side/thrill_seekers_1.

24. Tanner Christensen, "Fear Isn't All Bad When It Comes to Creativity," *Create Something*, October 27, 2015, http://creativesomething.net /post/131684346839/creativity-is-the-same-no-matter-the-topic.

25. "Fear of Crime Can Have a Positive Effect Too, Argues New Study," *London School of Economics and Political Science*, May 24, 2011, http:// www.lse.ac.uk/newsAndMedia/news/archives/2009/08/functional fear.aspx.

26. Alice Park, "Here's How to Make Waiting a Little Less Excruciating," *Time*, December 5, 2014, http://time.com/3619146/wait-more -patiently/.

27. Kim Masters, "The Unorthodox Relationship between Kathryn Bigelow and Mark Boal," *Hollywood Reporter*, December 19, 2012, http:// www.hollywoodreporter.com/news/zero-dark-thirty-kathryn-bige low-404485.

28. "John Donne," Poetry Foundation, http://www.poetryfoundation .org/bio/john-donne.

29. John Donne, "Farewell to Love," stanza 1, line 6.

30. Lauren Collins, "Christian Louboutin and the Psychology of Shoes," *New Yorker*, March 28, 2011, http://www.newyorker.com/magazine /2011/03/28/sole-mate.

31. Emma Hope Allwood, "Fashion's Most Extreme Footwear," *Dazed*, n.d., http://www.dazeddigital.com/fashion/article/22849/1/fashion-s -most-extreme-footwear.

32. Ella Alexander, "YSL Closes Louboutin Court Case," *Vogue*, October 16, 2012, http://www.vogue.co.uk/article/christian-louboutin -sues-yves-saint-laurent-for-red-sole-shoes.

33. Melissa Quinones, "11 White Celebs That Love Using The N-Word (LIST)," *Global Grind*, 2013, http://globalgrind.com/2013 /08/02/white-celebrities-that-have-used-said-the-n-word-list/.

34. Jessie Heyman, "13 Stars Who Went to Extreme Lengths for Movie Roles," *Vogue*, December 22, 2015, http://www.vogue.com/13230885 /actors-who-go-to-extreme-lengths/.

35. Nathan Gibson, "11 of the Most Extreme Measures Taken by Actors for a Role," *The Richest*, March 7, 2015, http://www.therichest.com

/expensive-lifestyle/entertainment/10-of-the-most-extreme-mea
sures-taken-by-actors-for-a-role/?view=all.

36. Laura Montini, "The Easiest Way to Promote Gender Equality at
Your Company," *Inc.*, January 13, 2015, http://www.inc.com/laura
-montini/why-your-meetings-should-probably-include-a-talking
-stick.html.

37. Sarah Watts, " 'Running the Gauntlet': The Internet's Most Disgusting Challenge," *Daily Beast*, October 27, 2015, http://www.thedai
lybeast.com/articles/2015/10/27/running-the-gauntlet-the-internet
-s-most-disgusting-challenge.html.

38. Jon Perr, "Studies Confirm the Closing of the Conservative Mind,"
Daily Kos, July 12, 2010, http://www.dailykos.com/story/2010/7/12
/883743/-.

39. Connor Wood, "The Age of Extreme Opinions," *Patheos*, December 24, 2014, http://www.patheos.com/blogs/scienceonreligion/2014
/12/the-age-of-extreme-opinions/.

40. Judith Butler, "Hannah Arendt's Challenge to Adolf Eichmann,"
The Guardian, August 29, 2011, http://www.theguardian.com/comment
isfree/2011/aug/29/hannah-arendt-adolf-eichmann-banality-of
-evil.

41. ABC News, "Restaurant Shift Turns into Nightmare," *ABC News*,
November 10, 2005, http://abcnews.go.com/Primetime/story?id
=1297922&page=1.

42. Andrew Wolfson, "A Hoax Most Cruel: Caller Coaxed McDonald's
Managers into Strip-Searching a Worker," *Courier Journal*, October 9,
2005, http://www.courier-journal.com/story/news/local/2005/10/09
/a-hoax-most-cruel-caller-coaxed-mcdonalds-managers-/28936597/.

43. Kenneth Worthy, "Are Polite People More Violent and Destructive?"
Psychology Today, June 23, 2014, https://www.psychologytoday.com
/blog/the-green-mind/201406/are-polite-people-more-violent-and
-destructive.

44. Katherine Harmon, "The Origin of Hatred," *Scientific American*, August 19, 2009, http://www.scientificamerican.com/article/the-origin
-of-hatred/.

45. Shona Ghosh, "Stop Optimising 'The Sh★t' Out of Marketing, Says
Adidas Brand Boss," *Campaign*, April 30, 2015, http://www.marketing

magazine.co.uk/article/1345296/stop-optimising-the-sht-market ing-says-adidas-brand-boss.

46. Vanessa Grigoriadis, "Riding High," *Vanity Fair*, August 15, 2012, http://www.vanityfair.com/hollywood/2012/09/soul-cycle -celebrity-cult-following.

47. Ibid.

Chapter 5: Flaws

1. John Harlow and Roya Nikkah, "US Declines to Go Ga-Ga over Royal Baby," *Sunday Times*, April 19, 2015, http://www.thesunday times.co.uk/sto/news/uk_news/article1545917.ece.

2. Stephanie Merry, "Drop the Photoshop: 'Girls' Creator Lena Dunham Wants Magazines to Stop 'Retouching' Her Photos," *Washington Post*, reprinted in *Star-Ledger* (New Jersey), March 9, 2016, 31.

3. H. Hennig, R. Fleischmann, A. Fredebohm, Y. Hagmayer, J. Nagler, A. Witt, et al., "The Nature and Perception of Fluctuations in Human Musical Rhythms," *PLOS One* 6, no. 10 (2011): e26457. doi:10.1371/ journal.pone.0026457.

4. E. Aronson, B. Willerman, and J. Floyd, "The Effect of a Pratfall on Increasing Interpersonal Attractiveness," *Psychonomic Science* 4, no. 6 (June 1966): 227–228, doi:10.3758/BF03342263.

5. Brené Brown, *The Gifts of Imperfection* (Center City, MN: Hazelden Publishing, 2010).

6. Peter D. Harms, Seth M. Spain, and Sean T. Hannah, "Leader Development and the Dark Side of Personality," *Leadership Quarterly* 22 (2011): 495–509. doi:10.1016/j.leaqua.2011.04.007, http://digital commons.unl.edu/managementfacpub/82/.

7. Matthew Biddle, "Study: Men Tend to Be More Narcissistic than Women," University at Buffalo News Center, SUNY, March 4, 2015, http://www.buffalo.edu/news/releases/2015/03/009.html.

8. Molly Young, "The J in J.Crew," *New York*, August 14, 2011, http:// nymag.com/fashion/11/fall/jenna-lyons/.

9. Lauren Sherman, "Our Top Ten Moments from J.Crew's Fall Presentation," *Fashionista*, April 4, 2010, http://fashionista.com/2010/04 /our-top-ten-favorite-moments-from-j-crews-fall-presentation.

10. "Jenna Lyons' Social Life Is the Least of J.Crew's Problems," *Yahoo*

Style, December 23, 2014, https://www.yahoo.com/style/jenna-lyons
-social-life-the-least-of-j-crews-105996929648.html.

11. Adrienne Sanders, "Charles O'Reilly: Narcissists Get Paid More than You Do," Insights by Stanford Business, July 14, 2014, https://www.gsb.stanford.edu/insights/charles-oreilly-narcissists-get-paid-more-you-do.

12. David Elkind, "Egocentrism in Adolescence," in *Readings in Developmental Psychology*, 2nd ed., ed. Judith Krieger Gardner and Ed Gardner (Boston: Little, Brown), 383–90.

13. "Suitors of Penelope," Greek Mythology Link, http://www.maicar.com/GML/SUITORSPENELOPE.html.

14. "Will 'Going Clear' Ruin Tom Cruise's Summer?" *USA Today*, May 5, 2015, http://www.usatoday.com/story/life/movies/2015/05/05/challenged-by-going-clear-another-test-awaits-tom-cruise/2694 1297/.

15. Kamau High, "Advocacy Group Blasts Unilever's 'Hypocrisy,'" *AdWeek*, October 11, 2007, http://www.adweek.com/news/advertising/advocacy-group-blasts-unilevers-hypocrisy-90630.

16. "L'Oréal Is Misleading Customers about Being Cruelty Free," *Cruelty-Free Kitty*, November 16, 2014, http://www.crueltyfreekitty.com/news/loreal-animal-testing-not-cruelty-free/.

Chapter 6: Intimate

1. Martin Booth, *A Magick Life: The Biography of Aleister Crowley* (London: Coronet Books, 2000), 15–16; Lawrence Sutin, *Do What Thou Wilt: A Life of Aleister Crowley* (New York: St. Martin's Press, 2000), 25–26; Richard Kaczynski, *Perdurabo: The Life of Aleister Crowley*, 2nd ed. (Berkeley, CA: North Atlantic Books, 2010), 23.

2. Booth, *Magick Life*, 26–27; Sutin, *Do What Thou Wilt*, 33; Kaczynski, *Perdurabo*, 24, 27; Tobias Churton, *Aleister Crowley: The Biography* (London: Watkins Books: 2011), 26.

3. Sutin, *Do What Thou Wilt*, 38.

4. Kaczynski, *Perdurabo*, 36.

5. Booth, *Magick Life*, 98–103.

6. Henrik Bogdan and Martin P. Starr, "Introduction," in *Aleister Crowley and Western Esotericism* (Oxford: Oxford University Press, 2012), 7.

7. Christopher M. Moreman, "Devil Music and the Great Beast: Ozzy Osbourne, Aleister Crowley, and the Christian Right," *Journal of Religion and Popular Culture* 3, no. 1 (2003).

8. Michael Musto, "Anonymous Sex in Steam Rooms: An Inside Report," *Village Voice*, January 15, 2013, http://www.villagevoice.com/blogs/anonymous-sex-in-steam-rooms-an-inside-report-6381001.

9. "9 Stellar Examples of the Unintended Use of Products," Printwand.com, http://www.printwand.com/blog/9-stellar-examples-of-the-unintended-use-of-products.

10. Megan Gambino, "A Salute to the Wheel," *Smithsonian* magazine, June 17, 2009, http://www.smithsonianmag.com/science-nature/a-salute-to-the-wheel-31805121/#G4ZstO2sImCywHT9.99.

11. Gabriel Paolo Ricafrente, "The Ancient and Surprising History of the Treadmill, Attendly.com, July 3, 2015, http://www.attendly.com/the-ancient-and-surprising-history-of-the-treadmill/.

12. Ibid.

13. Karley Sciortino, "Breathless: Is UberPool the New Tinder?" *Vogue*, September 24, 2015, http://www.vogue.com/13352052/breathless-karley-sciortino-uberpool/.

14. Maggie M. K. Hess. "Dear Fellow Rider, Using Uberpool to Pick Up Dates Is Creepy." *Washington Post*, September 24, 2015, https://www.washingtonpost.com/news/soloish/wp/2015/09/24/uberpool-is-not-your-private-dating-service/.

15. Diane Berenbaum, "Four Key Strategies for Building Emotional Connections with Your Customers," Communico, http://www.communicoltd.com/pages/1076_four_key_strategies_for_building_emotional_connections_with_your_customers.cfm

16. Nichole Tucker, "Popular Game Tetris Proven to Reduce Addictions, Cravings [Study]," *Inquistr*, August 15, 2015, http://www.inquisitr.com/2337585/popular-game-tetris-proven-to-reduce-addiction-cravings-study/

17. Indo-Asian News Service, "Playing Tetris Can Help Reduce Craving for Drugs, Food, and Sex: Study," *Gadgets 360*, August 17, 2015, http://gadgets.ndtv.com/games/news/playing-tetris-can-help-reduce-craving-for-drugs-food-and-sex-study-728802.

18. "'Out-of-Body' Virtual Experience Could Help Social Anxiety,"

Neuroscience News, June 23, 2014, http://neurosciencenews.com/cyber psychology-virtual-imaging-social-anxiety-257/.

19. " 'Out-of-Body' Virtual Experience."

20. "Virtual Reality," http://www0.cs.ucl.ac.uk/research/vr/Projects /SocialPhobias/research.htm.

21. Alex Senson, "Virtual Reality Therapy: Treating the Global Mental Health Crisis," *TechCrunch*, January 6, 2016, http://techcrunch.com /2016/01/06/virtual-reality-therapy-treating-the-global-mental -health-crisis/.

22. Anu Leppiman, "Young Consumers and Their Brand Love," *International Journal of Business and Social Research* 5, no. 10 (2015).

23. B. Schmitt, "The Consumer Psychology of Brands," *Journal of Consumer Psychology* 22 (2012): 7–17.

24. Brené Brown, "The Power of Vulnerability," TED Talk, YouTube, January 3, 2011, https://www.youtube.com/watch?v=iCvmsMzlF7o &feature=share.

25. Betsy Prioleau, *Seductress: Women Who Ravished the World and Their Lost Art of Love* (New York: Viking, 2003), 168.

26. Ibid., 168, 169.

27. Ibid., 171, 170.

28. "Biography," official site of Josephine Baker, http://www.cmgww .com/stars/baker/about/biography.html.

29. Ibid.

30. Prioleau, *Seductress*, 171.

31. "Biography."

32. Prioleau, *Seductress*, 172.

33. Aria Hughes, "2(x)ist Unveils Women's Collection," *WWD*, October 27, 2015, http://wwd.com/markets-news/intimates-activewear /2xist-womens-10269542/.

34. "2(x)ist Unveils Women's Collection," *MAGIC Online*, October 27, 2015, http://www.magiconline.com/news/2xist-unveils-womens -collection.

35. Ibid.

36. Jase Peeples, "UPDATE: Rose McGowan Blasts Gay Community," *Advocate*, November 5, 2014, http://www.advocate.com/arts-enter tainment/people/2014/11/05/rose-mcgowan-blasts-gay-community.

37. Kristopher Fraser, "2(x)ist Attempting to Become Complete Lifestyle

Brand," *Fashion United*, April 23, 2015, https://fashionunited.com /news/retail/2-x-ist-attempting-to-become-complete-lifestyle-brand /201504236734.

38. H. E. Fisher, *Anatomy of Love* (New York: W.W. Norton, 1992).

39. H. E. Fisher, "Serial Monogamy and Clandestine Adultery: Evolution and Consequences of the Dual Human Reproductive Strategy," in *Applied Evolutionary Psychology*, ed. S. C. Roberts (New York: Oxford University Press, 2011).

40. Steven W. Gangestad and Randy Thornhill, "The Evolutionary Psychology of Extrapair Sex: The Role of Fluctuating Asymmetry," *Evolution and Human Behavior* 18, no. 2 (March 1997): 69–88, doi: http://dx.doi.org/10.1016/S1090-5138(97)00003-2.

41. Quoted in Fisher, "Serial Monogamy."

42. William Jankowiak and Helen Gerth, "Can You Love More than One Person at the Same Time?" research report, University of Nevada.

43. D. Anapol, *Polyamory: The New Love without Limits; Secrets of Sustainable Intimate Relationships* (San Rafael, CA: IntiNet Resource Center, 1997); L. Kipnis, "Adultery," in *Intimacy*, ed. Lauren Berlant (Chicago: University of Chicago Press, 2000), 9–47; L. Wolfe, "Jealousy and Transformation in Polyamorous Relationships," dissertation, Institute of Advanced Study of Human Sexuality, San Francisco, 2003.

44. "Valeria Lukyanova," *Wikipedia*, last modified August 10, 2016, https://en.wikipedia.org/wiki/Valeria_Lukyanova.

45. "Justin Jedlica," *Wikipedia*, last modified August 14, 2016, https://en .wikipedia.org/wiki/Justin_Jedlica.

46. Craig A. Williams, *Roman Homosexuality*, 2nd ed. (Oxford: Oxford University Press, 2010), 284.

47. Ibid., 285.

48. Jo Macfarlane, "Would YOU Pay £4,000 for Duran Duran's Anti-wrinkle Moisturiser? New Romantic Legend Nick Rhodes Has Joined Leading DNA Experts to Create an Eye-Wateringly Expensive Cream to Fight Ageing," *Daily Mail*, last modified May 3, 2015, http:// www.dailymail.co.uk/health/article-3065456/Would-pay-4-000 -Duran-Duran-s-anti-wrinkle-moisturiser-New-Romantic-legend -Nick-Rhodes-joined-leading-DNA-experts-create-eye-wateringly -expensive-cream-fight-ageing.html.

49. Divine Caroline, "DNA-Based Beauty Products: The Future of Skincare?" SkinDNA, 2012, http://www.skindna.com.au/divine.html.

50. Elizabeth Spaulding and Christopher Perry, "Making It Personal: Rules for Success in Product Customization," Bain and Company, September 16, 2013, http://www.bain.com/publications/articles/making -it-personal-rules-for-success-in-product-customization.aspx.

51. Nina Combs, "What DNA Taught Me about Diet and Exercise," *Men's Fitness*, October 14, 2014, http://www.mensfitness.com/weight-loss /burn-fat-fast/what-dna-test-taught-me-about-diet-and-exercise; Gene Trainer, https://www.genetrainer.com; "DNA Supplements May Be Secret of Longer, Healthier Life," *Genotopia*, http://genotopia .scienceblog.com/406/dna-supplements-may-be-secret-of-longer -healthier-life/.

52. Spaulding and Perry, "Making It Personal."

53. Liraz Margalit, "The Psychology of Online Customization," *Psychology Today*, March 13, 2015, https://www.psychologytoday.com/blog /behind-online-behavior/201503/the-psychology-online-customi zation.

54. Ibid.

55. Liraz Margalit, "The Psychology of Online Customization," *TechCrunch*, November 11, 2014, http://techcrunch.com/2014/11/11/the -rise-of-online-customization/.

56. Margalit, "Psychology of Online Customization."

Chapter 7: Execute

1. Lydia Dishman, "Millennials Have a Different Definition of Diversity and Inclusion," *FastCompany*, May 18, 2015, http://www.fast company.com/3046358/the-new-rules-of-work/millennials-have-a -different-definition-of-diversity-and-inclusion.

2. Jane Herman, "How to Harness the Powers of Negative Emotions," witi.com, http://www.witi.com/wire/articles/132/How-to-Harness -the-Powers-of-Negative-Emotions/.

3. Cari Sommer, "When You've Got It—Flaunt It: A Case Study on Marie Forleo," *Forbes*, February 22, 2012, http://www.forbes.com/sites /carisommer/2012/02/22/when-youve-got-it-flaunt-it-a-case-study -on-marie-forleo/#2b3e8ce0436c.

4. Maurice Smith, "Are You Ready for Generation Z?" LinkedIn, April 2,

2015, https://www.linkedin.com/pulse/you-ready-generation-z-mau rice-smith.

5. Sommer, "When You've Got It."

6. Susan Gunelius, "Be Your Own Brand Champion—Or Get One Now," *Forbes*, July 12, 2011, http://www.forbes.com/sites/work-in -progress/2011/07/12/be-your-own-brand-champion-or-get-one -now/#4de24b056584.

7. Peter Bregman, "The Right Way to Speak to Yourself," *Harvard Business Review*, August 27, 2012, https://hbr.org/2012/08/teach-yourself -to-have-a-healthy.html.

8. Propoint, "Six Tips to Telling a Better Business Story," *Forbes*, October 16, 2015, http://www.forbes.com/sites/propointgraphics/2015/10 /16/6-tips-to-telling-a-better-business-story/#2d7abb363109.

9. Neil Patel, "How to Tell Your Brand Story to the World," *Forbes*, December 3, 2014, http://www.forbes.com/sites/neilpatel/2014/12/03 /how-to-tell-your-brand-story-to-the-world/2/#3d8270d42bdd.

10. Jeremy Kingsley, "Don't Go to Work without Your Passion," *Fox Business*, May 24, 2013, http://www.foxbusiness.com/features/2013/05 /24/dont-go-to-work-without-your-passion.html.

11. Nick Morgan, "What Is Charisma? Can You Increase Your Own?" *Forbes*, February 2, 2016, http://www.forbes.com/sites/nickmorgan /2016/02/02/what-is-charisma-can-you-increase-your-own/#2b4 d585054fc.

12. Xueming Luo, Michael Wiles, and Sascha Raithel, "Make the Most of a Polarizing Brand," *Harvard Business Review*, November 2013, https://hbr.org/2013/11/make-the-most-of-a-polarizing-brand.

13. Austin Carr, " 'Twisted and Mischaracterized': How FanDuel's CEO Is Fighting Back against Detractors," *Fast Company*, April 18, 2016, http://www.fastcompany.com/3058506/twisted-and-mischara cterized-how-fanduels-ceo-is-fighting-back-against-detractors.

14. Capital One SparkVoice, "Catching a Buzz: Customers Can Be Your Best Marketers," *Forbes*, June 24, 2013, http://www.forbes.com/sites /capitalonespark/2013/06/24/catching-a-buzz-customers-can-be -your-best-marketers/#974ae191d49c.

15. Peter Bregman, "How to Escape Perfectionism," *Harvard Business Review*, September 1, 2009, https://hbr.org/2009/09/how-to-escape -perfectionism.

16. Mara Glatzel, "Having Your Own Back: Self-Love & Business," *Mara Glatzel*, January 31, 2014, http://www.maraglatzel.com/risk-imper fection-self-love-business/.

17. Michael Shermer, "The Mind's Compartments Create Conflicting Beliefs," *Scientific American*, January 1, 2013, http://www.scientific american.com/article/the-minds-compartments-create-conflicting -beliefs/.

Index

GET THE PRINCIPLE? STAY IN TOUCH!

Twitter: @JeetendrSehdev

Instagram: @Jeetendr_Sehdev

Snapchat: Jeetendr Sehdev

Linked In: Jeetendr Sehdev